어린 왕자 영어 필사

지은이 앙투안 드 생텍쥐페리
엮은이 서메리
펴낸이 임상진
펴낸곳 (주)넥서스

초판 1쇄 발행 2022년 10월 5일
초판 5쇄 발행 2024년 11월 1일

출판신고 1992년 4월 3일 제311-2002-2호
10880 경기도 파주시 지목로 5
Tel (02)330-5500 Fax (02)330-5555

ISBN 979-11-6683-329-8 13740

www.nexusbook.com

읽고 쓰며 가슴에 새기는

어린 왕자
영어
필사

앙투안 드 생텍쥐페리 원작
서메리 엮음

It is only with the heart that one can see rightly;
what is essential is invisible to the eye.

넥서스

어떤 책이 시대를 뛰어넘는 메시지를 전할 때, 우리는 그 작품을 고전이라 부른다. 반세기 전에 창조된 어린 왕자의 말들이 여전히 수많은 독자들의 마음을 울리는 건, 어쩌면 황금빛 머리칼을 지닌 그 아이의 시선이 누구나 보고 있지만 대부분은 눈치 채지 못한 삶의 본질을 정확히 꿰뚫고 있기 때문일 것이다.

If you come at four o'clock in the afternoon, then at three o'clock I shall begin to be happy.
만약 네가 오후 네 시에 온다면 난 세 시부터 행복해지기 시작할 거야.
What makes the desert beautiful is that somewhere it hides a well.
사막이 아름다운 건 어딘가에 샘을 숨기고 있기 때문이야.
What is essential is invisible to the eye.
중요한 건 눈에 보이지 않아.

친숙함을 넘어 당연하게까지 느껴지는 이 문장들이 『어린 왕자』 이전에는 존재하지 않았다는 사실을 떠올리면 새삼 경이로움이 밀려온다. 평소에는 의식조차 못하지만 사실은 매 순간 우리에게 생명을 불어넣는 공기와 같이, 시대를 관통하는 고전은 골똘히 생각하지 않아도 매 순간 우리의 마음을 풍요롭게 한다.

필사는 이러한 고전의 가치를 보다 깊이 체험하는 가장 좋은 방법 중 하나이다.

수없이 반복해서 읽은 책이라도 막상 그 문장들을 글로 써 보면 전혀 다른 느낌으로 다가 온다. 글자 하나, 조사 하나, 심지어 구두점 하나까지도 저마다의 의미를 품고 우리의 눈과 마음에 각인된다. 필사를 통해 좋은 책을 오롯이 소화한다면 삶을 바라보는 시선은 변화한다. 뛰어난 작가들이 하나같이 명작 필사의 중요성을 강조하는 것은 단순히 문장력을 키우라는 의미가 아닐 것이다.

『어린 왕자』를 우리말로 옮기고 필사할 문장을 고르는 과정에서 가장 신경 썼던 부분은 독자들의 경험이 단순한 '독해'에서 끝나지 않도록 하는 것이었다. 각 문장의 의미를 정확히 이해하면서도 글맛의 아름다움을 느낄 수 있도록, 원문의 길이와 구조를 유지하는 동시에 생생한 표현과 유려한 묘사를 최대한 살리려고 노력했다. 사전을 찾느라 독서의 흐름이 끊기지 않도록 중요한 단어들은 아래쪽에 따로 모아 배치했다.

이 책을 작업하는 과정은 즐거우면서도 한편으로 괴로움의 연속이었다. 시간 여유가 있는 사람이라면 전체를 통째로 읽고 써 보라고 권하고 싶을 정도로, 『어린 왕자』는 한 줄 한 줄이 명대사이자 명문장인 작품이다. 독자들의 수고를 덜어 주기 위해서라고는 하지만, 페이지를 가득 메운 주옥같은 문장을 추려 내는 작업이 결코 쉽지만은 않았다. 문장을 고를 때는 글 자체로 아름다우면서도, 필사한 내용을 읽었을 때 스토리가 연결될 수 있도록 한다는 기준을 잡고 구성했다.

잘 알려진 것과 같이, 『어린 왕자』는 생텍쥐페리의 자전적 경험이 녹아든 소설이다. 그는 비행기를 몰고 국경을 넘나드는 조종사였으며, 실제로 사하라 사막에 불시착하여 조난당한 적도 있다. 다른 별에서 왔다는 소년의 존재가 마냥 비현실적으로 느껴지지 않는 건 그저 작가의 필력 때문만이 아닐 것이다. 그의 배경을 알고 이 책을 읽은 사람은 누구나 이런 생각을 떠올린다. 어쩌면 생텍쥐페리가 사하라 사막에서 헤매던 5일 동안 정말로 어린 왕자를 만났을지 모른다고.

『어린 왕자』의 마지막은 다음과 같은 문장으로 마무리된다.

If a little man appears, send me word that he has come back.
어린 왕자가 나타난다면 내게 그가 돌아왔다는 소식을 전해 주길 부탁한다.

『어린 왕자』를 출간한 이듬해, 생텍쥐페리는 비행기 조종 중에 실종되었다. 그리고 끝까지 발견되지 않았다. 그는 어린 왕자를 만나러 갔을까? 언제까지나 어린 아이의 모습을 간직한 친구와 함께 장미와 양을 돌보며 바오바브나무 새싹을 뽑고 있을까?

독자 여러분이 필사라는 통로를 통해 두 사람의 순수한 우정에 동참하는 행복을 누리길 바란다. 아름다운 문장과 날카로운 통찰이 한데 엮인 어린 왕자의 말들을 한 글자 한 글자 마음에 새기길 바란다. 그 시간을 통해 살아오며 조금쯤 잃어버렸을지 모를 자신의 순수함을 되찾을 수 있을 것이다.

All grown-ups were once children.
모든 어른에게는 어린이였던 시절이 있었다.

서메리

「어린 왕자 영어 필사」100% 활용법

하루 10분 매일 영어 필사 루틴

1. 서메리 작가가 낭독하는 「어린 왕자」를 듣는다.
2. 서메리 작가가 선별한 명문장을 필사한다.
3. 「어린 왕자」 원어민 MP3를 수시로 듣는다.

서메리 작가
영상 바로 보기

MP3 무료로 다운받기

1 **www.nexusbook.com**에서
도서명으로 검색하여 다운받으세요.

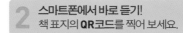

2 스마트폰에서 바로 듣기!
책 표지의 **QR코드**를 찍어 보세요.

저자 낭독 &
원어민 MP3

TO LEON WERTH

I ask the indulgence of the children who may read this book for dedicating it to a grown-up. I have a serious reason: he is the best friend I have in the world. I have another reason: this grown-up understands everything, even books about children. I have a third reason: he lives in France where he is hungry and cold. He needs cheering up. If all these reasons are not enough, I will dedicate the book to the child from whom this grown-up grew. All grown-ups were once children--although few of them remember it. And so I correct my dedication:

TO LEON WERTH
WHEN HE WAS A LITTLE BOY

어휘 indulgence 관용 dedicate 바치다 grown-up 어른 reason 이유 cheer up 기운을 북돋우다 enough 충분한 although 비록 ~이지만 correct 정정하다

I ask the indulgence of the children who may read this book for dedicating it to a grown-up.

If all these reasons are not enough, I will dedicate the book to the child from whom this grown-up grew.

All grown-ups were once children--although few of them remember it.

레옹 베르트에게

이 책을 어른에게 바치는 것에 대해 어린이 여러분의 용서를 바란다. 여기에는 중요한 이유가 있다. 이 어른은 이 세상에서 나와 가장 친한 친구이다. 또 다른 이유는 이 어른이 세상 모든 것을, 어린이를 위한 책까지도 이해하는 사람이라는 것이다. 세 번째 이유는 이 어른이 지금 프랑스에서 지내고 있으며, 추위와 굶주림에 떨고 있다는 점이다. 그에게는 위로가 필요하다. 만약 이 모든 이유로도 부족하다면 한때 어린이였던 그에게 이 책을 바치도록 하겠다. 비록 그 사실을 기억하는 사람은 거의 없지만, 모든 어른에게는 어린이였던 시절이 있었다. 그렇다면 이 헌사를 이렇게 고쳐야 할 것 같다.

어린 소년이었던 시절의 레옹 베르트에게

The Little Prince

1

Once when I was six years old I saw a magnificent picture in a book, called *True Stories from Nature*, about the primeval forest. It was a picture of a boa constrictor in the act of swallowing an animal. Here is a copy of the drawing.

In the book it said: "Boa constrictors swallow their prey whole, without chewing it. After that they are not able to move, and they sleep through the six months that they need for digestion."

I pondered deeply, then, over the adventures of the jungle. And after some work with a colored pencil I succeeded in making my first drawing. My Drawing Number One. It looked something like this:

---

 magnificent 감명 깊은   primeval forest 원시림   boa constrictor(a) 보아뱀
swallow 삼키다   prey 먹이   chew 씹다   digestion 소화   ponder 생각하다

I saw a magnificent picture in a book, called *True Stories from Nature*, about the primeval forest.

I pondered deeply, then, over the adventures of the jungle.

And after some work with a colored pencil I succeeded in making my first drawing.

여섯 살 때, 나는 원시림의 이야기를 다룬 『자연의 진실』이라는 책에서 엄청난 삽화를 보았다. 그것은 맹수를 집어삼키는 보아뱀의 그림이었다. 아래는 그 그림을 옮겨 그린 것이다. 그 책에는 이렇게 쓰여 있었다. "보아뱀은 먹이를 씹지 않고 통째로 삼킨다. 그러고 나면 몸을 움직일 수 없기 때문에 6개월 동안 잠을 자며 소화를 시킨다." 나는 정글에서 벌어지는 모험들에 대해 곰곰이 생각한 뒤 색연필을 가지고 인생 첫 번째 그림을 성공적으로 그려냈다. 나의 그림 1호였다. 그것은 아래와 같이 생겼다.

I showed my masterpiece to the grown-ups, and asked them whether the drawing frightened them.

But they answered: "Frighten? Why should any one be frightened by a hat?"

My drawing was not a picture of a hat. It was a picture of a boa constrictor digesting an elephant. But since the grown-ups were not able to understand it, I made another drawing: I drew the inside of a boa constrictor, so that the grown-ups could see it clearly. They always need to have things explained. My Drawing Number Two looked like this:

어휘 **masterpiece** 명작, 걸작 **whether** ~인지 아닌지 **answer** 대답하다 **frighten** 겁먹게 만들다 **digest** 소화시키다 **understand** 이해하다 **clearly** 정확하게 **explain** 설명하다

I showed my masterpiece to the grown-ups, and asked them whether the drawing frightened them.

But they answered: "Frighten? Why should any one be frightened by a hat?"

They always need to have things explained. My Drawing Number Two looked like this:

나는 이 명작을 어른들에게 보여 주면서 무섭지 않냐고 물었다. 하지만 어른들은 이렇게 대답했다. "무섭냐고? 모자를 무서워하는 사람이 어디 있니?" 내 그림은 모자가 아니었다. 그것은 코끼리를 소화시키고 있는 보아뱀의 모습이었다. 하지만 어른들은 이해하지 못했고, 나는 그들이 정확히 알 수 있도록 보아뱀의 배 속을 그렸다. 어른들은 모든 것을 설명해 주어야 한다. 나의 그림 2호는 다음과 같았다.

The grown-ups' response, this time, was to advise me to lay aside my drawings of boa constrictors, whether from the inside or the outside, and devote myself instead to geography, history, arithmetic, and grammar. That is why, at the age of six, I gave up what might have been a magnificent career as a painter. I had been disheartened by the failure of my Drawing Number One and my Drawing Number Two. Grown-ups never understand anything by themselves, and it is tiresome for children to be always and forever explaining things to them.

So then I chose another profession, and learned to pilot airplanes. I have flown a little over all parts of the world; and it is true that geography has been very useful to me. At a glance I can distinguish China from Arizona. If one gets lost in the night, such knowledge is valuable.

어휘 advise 조언하다 lay aside 포기하다 devote 바치다 geography 지리학
arithmetic 산수 dishearten 낙담하게 하다 tiresome 성가신 glance 흘낏 보다
distinguish 구분하다

It is tiresome for children to be always and forever explaining things to them.

I have flown a little over all parts of the world; and it is true that geography has been very useful to me.

If one gets lost in the night, such knowledge is valuable.

이번에 어른들이 보인 반응은, 속이 보이든 보이지 않든 보아뱀의 그림 따위는 집어치우고 지리나 역사, 수학, 문법에 관심을 가지라는 것이었다. 그래서 나는 여섯 살 나이에 화가라는 멋진 직업을 포기해버렸다. 그림 1호와 2호가 전부 실패를 거둔 데 낙담했던 것이다. 어른들은 결코 스스로 이해하는 법을 몰랐고, 그럴 때마다 모든 것을 일일이 설명해 주어야 한다는 건 어린이로서 너무 피곤한 일이었다. 결국 다른 직업을 택해야 했던 나는 비행기 조종을 배웠고, 세계 곳곳을 빠짐없이 누볐다. 지리는 나에게 실제로 매우 유용한 과목이었다. 나는 중국과 애리조나 땅을 슬쩍 보기만 해도 구분할 수 있었다. 이런 능력은 야간 비행 도중 길을 잃어버렸을 때 큰 도움이 되었다.

In the course of this life I have had a great many encounters with a great many people who have been concerned with matters of consequence. I have lived a great deal among grown-ups. I have seen them intimately, close at hand. And that hasn't much improved my opinion of them.

Whenever I met one of them who seemed to me at all clear-sighted, I tried the experiment of showing him my Drawing Number One, which I have always kept. I would try to find out, so, if this was a person of true understanding. But, whoever it was, he, or she, would always say:

"That is a hat."

Then I would never talk to that person about boa constrictors, or primeval forests, or stars. I would bring myself down to his level. I would talk to him about bridge, and golf, and politics, and neckties. And the grown-up would be greatly pleased to have met such a sensible man.

어휘 encounter 만나다 be concerned with ~에 관심이 있다 a matter of consequence 중요한 일 intimately 밀접하게 opinion 의견 clear-sighted 명석한 experiment 실험 bridge 브리지(카드 게임) politics 정치 sensible 분별력 있는

I have had a great many encounters with a great many people who have been concerned with matters of consequence.

_____

_____

I tried the experiment of showing him my Drawing Number One, which I have always kept.

_____

_____

And the grown-up would be greatly pleased to have met such a sensible man.

_____

_____

해석

이렇게 살아가는 동안, 나는 일의 중요도를 따지는 사람들과 수없는 만남을 가졌다. 어른들 틈에서 오랫동안 지내온 것이다. 그들을 가까운 거리에서 자세히 관찰했지만, 어른에 대한 평가는 별로 나아지지 않았다. 조금이라도 똑똑해 보이는 사람을 만나면, 나는 항상 지니고 다니던 그림 1호를 보여 주며 그를 시험했다. 상대가 보이는 것을 진정으로 이해할 수 있는 사람인지 알고 싶었다. 하지만 남자든 여자든, 항상 이렇게 말했다. "모자군요." 그러면 나는 보아뱀이나 원시림, 별에 대한 이야기를 입에 담지 않았다. 대신 그가 이해할 수 있는 이야기를 꺼냈다. 브리지게임이나 골프, 정치, 넥타이 같은 이야기 말이다. 그러면 그 어른은 분별 있는 청년을 알게 되었다며 매우 기뻐했다.

So I lived my life alone, without anyone that I could really talk to, until I had an accident with my plane in the Desert of Sahara, six years ago. Something was broken in my engine. And as I had with me neither a mechanic nor any passengers, I set myself to attempt the difficult repairs all alone. It was a question of life or death for me: I had scarcely enough drinking water to last a week.

The first night, then, I went to sleep on the sand, a thousand miles from any human habitation. I was more isolated than a shipwrecked sailor on a raft in the middle of the ocean. Thus you can imagine my amazement, at sunrise, when I was awakened by an odd little voice. It said:

"If you please--draw me a sheep!"

"What!"

"Draw me a sheep!"

---

 alone 혼자 accident 사고 desert 사막 mechanic 정비사 passenger 승객
repair 수리하다 scarcely 거의 없다 habitation 거주지 isolate 고립시키다
shipwreck 난파 raft 뗏목 odd 이상한

So I lived my life alone, without anyone that I could really talk to,

_____

_____

And as I had with me neither a mechanic nor any passengers, I set myself to attempt the difficult repairs all alone.

_____

_____

Thus you can imagine my amazement, at sunrise, when I was awakened by an odd little voice.

_____

_____

그렇게 나는 마음 터놓을 친구 하나 없이 홀로 지내왔다. 6년 전, 사하라 사막에서 비행기가 고장을 일으키기 전까지는. 엔진 부품이 망가졌는데 정비사도 승객도 없는 상황이었으므로, 나 혼자 까다로운 수리 작업을 준비해야 했다. 그것은 죽느냐 사느냐의 문제였다. 남은 물은 일주일쯤 버틸까 말까 한 정도였다. 첫날 밤, 나는 사람이 사는 지역에서 수천 킬로미터 떨어진 사막에서 잠이 들었다. 망망대해에 난파된 뗏목에 있는 선원보다도 더욱 고립된 상태였다. 그러니 해가 뜰 무렵 작고 이상한 목소리가 나를 깨웠을 때 내가 얼마나 놀랐겠는가. "저기…. 양 한 마리만 그려 줄래?" "뭐?" "양을 그려 줘!"

I jumped to my feet, completely thunderstruck. I blinked my eyes hard. I looked carefully all around me. And I saw a most extraordinary small person, who stood there examining me with great seriousness. Here you may see the best portrait that, later, I was able to make of him. But my drawing is certainly very much less charming than its model.

That, however, is not my fault. The grown-ups discouraged me in my painter's career when I was six years old, and I never learned to draw anything, except boas from the outside and boas from the inside.

어휘 completely 완전히 thunderstruck 벼락을 맞은 듯한 blink 깜빡이다 extraordinary 기이한 examine 조사하다 seriousness 심각함 portrait 초상화 charming 매력적인 discourage 낙담시키다

20

I saw a most extraordinary small person, who stood there examining me with great seriousness.

Here you may see the best portrait that, later, I was able to make of him.

I never learned to draw anything, except boas from the outside and boas from the inside.

나는 벼락이라도 맞은 듯 후다닥 일어나 눈을 끔뻑거리며 주변을 둘러보았다. 그러자 아주 심각한 얼굴로 나를 관찰하고 있던, 정말이지 신기한 생김새의 조그마한 사람이 눈에 들어왔다. 훗날 내가 그린 그의 초상화 중에서 가장 잘 된 작품을 여기 소개한다. 하지만 이 그림은 실제 모델보다 훨씬 덜 매력적이다. 어쨌거나 그건 내 잘못이 아니다. 어른들이 화가로서의 내 경력을 좌절시킨 여섯 살 전후로 그림 그리는 법을 전혀 배우지 않았으니까. 내가 그려 본 그림이라곤 속이 보이거나 보이지 않는 보아뱀뿐이었다.

Now I stared at this sudden apparition with my eyes fairly starting out of my head in astonishment. Remember, I had crashed in the desert a thousand miles from any inhabited region. And yet my little man seemed neither to be straying uncertainly among the sands, nor to be fainting from fatigue or hunger or thirst or fear. Nothing about him gave any suggestion of a child lost in the middle of the desert, a thousand miles from any human habitation. When at last I was able to speak, I said to him:

"But--what are you doing here?"

And in answer he repeated, very slowly, as if he were speaking of a matter of great consequence:

"If you please--draw me a sheep..."

When a mystery is too overpowering, one dare not disobey. Absurd as it might seem to me, a thousand miles from any human habitation and in danger of death, I took out of my pocket a sheet of paper and my fountain-pen.

 apparition 유령 astonishment 깜짝 놀람 inhabited (사람이) 거주하는 region 지역
stray 위치를 벗어나다 fatigue 피로 overpowering 아주 강한 disobey 불복종하다
fountain-pen 만년필

Now I stared at this sudden apparition with my eyes fairly starting out of my head in astonishment.

And yet my little man seemed neither to be straying uncertainly among the sands, nor to be fainting from fatigue or hunger or thirst or fear.

나는 생각지도 못하게 나타난 유령의 존재에 너무 놀라서 눈이 튀어나올 듯 그를 바라보았다. 기억하시라. 나는 사람이 사는 지역에서 수천 킬로미터 떨어진 장소에 있었다. 그런데 이 어린 소년은 길을 잃은 것 같지도 않았고, 피로나 배고픔, 목마름이나 두려움에 시달리는 것 같지도 않았다. 사람이 사는 지역에서 수천 킬로미터 떨어진 사막 한가운데서 길을 잃은 어린아이 같은 느낌이 전혀 없었다. 가까스로 말문이 트였을 때, 나는 그에게 물었다. "그런데, 너는 여기서 뭘 하고 있니?" 그는 매우 중요한 문제라도 얘기하듯 느린 속도로 했던 말을 반복했다. "양 한 마리만 그려 줘." 너무나 압도적인 신비가 닥쳐오면 인간은 순순히 상황을 따르게 된다. 사람이 사는 지역에서 수천 킬로미터 떨어진 곳에서 죽음의 위협을 마주한 사람으로서 정말 엉뚱한 짓이라는 생각이 들었지만, 나는 주머니에서 종이와 만년필을 꺼내 들었다.

But then I remembered how my studies had been concentrated on geography, history, arithmetic and grammar, and I told the little chap (a little crossly, too) that I did not know how to draw. He answered me:

"That doesn't matter. Draw me a sheep..."

But I had never drawn a sheep. So I drew for him one of the two pictures I had drawn so often. It was that of the boa constrictor from the outside. And I was astounded to hear the little fellow greet it with,

"No, no, no! I do not want an elephant inside a boa constrictor. A boa constrictor is a very dangerous creature, and an elephant is very cumbersome. Where I live, everything is very small. What I need is a sheep. Draw me a sheep."

 concentrate on ~에 집중하다 chap 녀석, 친구 crossly 퉁명스럽게 matter 중요하다
dangerous 위험한 creature 생명체 cumbersome 크고 무거운

I told the little chap that I did not know how to draw.

A boa constrictor is a very dangerous creature, and an elephant is very cumbersome.

Where I live, everything is very small.

그러나 별안간 내가 살면서 공부한 거라곤 지리와 역사, 수학, 문법뿐이라는 사실이 생각났다. 나는 그 꼬마 친구에게 (다소 퉁명스러운 말투로) 그림을 그릴 줄 모른다고 대꾸했다. 그는 대답했다. "그런 건 중요하지 않아. 양을 한 마리 그려 줘." 하지만 생전 양을 그려 본 적이 없으므로, 나는 그에게 내가 자주 그렸던 두 가지의 그림 중 하나를 그려 주었다. 그것은 속이 보이지 않는 보아뱀 그림이었다. 그런데 그 꼬마 친구가 이렇게 대답하는 게 아닌가. "아니야, 이게 아니야! 보아뱀 배 속에 들어 있는 코끼리는 싫어. 보아뱀은 아주 위험한 생물이고 코끼리는 너무 커. 내가 사는 곳은 모든 것이 아주 작아. 내게 필요한 건 양이야. 그러니까 양을 그려 줘."

So then I made a drawing.

He looked at it carefully, then he said:

"No. This sheep is already very sickly.
Make me another."

So I made another drawing.

My friend smiled gently and indulgently.

"You see yourself," he said, "that this is
not a sheep. This is a ram. It has horns."

So then I did my drawing over once
more.

어휘 carefully 신중하게 sickly 병약한 another 또 하나 smile 미소 짓다 indulgently
너그럽게 ram 숫양 horn 뿔

So then I made a drawing.

"No. This sheep is already very sickly. Make me another."

My friend smiled gently and indulgently.

그래서 나는 양을 그렸다. 그는 내 그림을 주의 깊게 바라보더니 말했다. "안 돼. 이 양은 벌써 병이 들었어.
다른 양을 그려 줘." 나는 다시 그림을 그렸다. 내 친구는 너그럽고 상냥한 미소를 지었다. "보다시피." 그가
말했다. "이건 그냥 양이 아니라 숫양이야. 뿔이 달렸잖아." 그래서 나는 또다시 그림을 그려 주었다.

But it was rejected too, just like the others.

"This one is too old. I want a sheep that will live a long time."

By this time my patience was exhausted, because I was in a hurry to start taking my engine apart. So I tossed off this drawing.

And I threw out an explanation with it.

어휘 reject 거절하다 patience 인내심 exhaust 고갈시키다 hurry 서두름 take apart 분해하다 toss off ~을 단숨에 만들어 내다 throw out 말하다, 내뱉다

"This one is too old. I want a sheep that will live a long time."

By this time my patience was exhausted, because I was in a hurry to start taking my engine apart.

So I tossed off this drawing.

하지만 이번에도 앞서와 마찬가지로 거절이었다. "이건 너무 늙었어. 난 오래 살 수 있는 양을 갖고 싶어." 이쯤 되자 내 인내심은 바닥났다. 내게는 당장 분해를 시작해야 하는 엔진이 있었다. 나는 아래와 같은 그림을 대충 끄적였다. 그리고 그에게 설명을 던졌다.

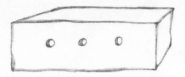

"This is only his box. The sheep you asked for is inside." I was very surprised to see a light break over the face of my young judge: "That is exactly the way I wanted it! Do you think that this sheep will have to have a great deal of grass?"

"Why?"

"Because where I live everything is very small..."

"There will surely be enough grass for him," I said. "It is a very small sheep that I have given you."

He bent his head over the drawing.

"Not so small that--Look! He has gone to sleep..."

And that is how I made the acquaintance of the little prince.

어휘 ask for ~를 요청하다 surprise 놀라게 하다 break over ~에 쏟아지다 judge 판사, 심사위원 grass 풀 bend 숙이다 acquaintance 친분

"This is only his box. The sheep you asked for is inside."

I was very surprised to see a light break over the face of my young judge.

And that is how I made the acquaintance of the little prince.

"이건 양이 담긴 상자야. 네가 원하는 양은 이 안에 들어 있어." 그 순간 내 작은 심사위원의 얼굴이 환하게 밝아지는 것을 보고 나는 깜짝 놀랐다. "이게 바로 내가 원하던 거야! 이 양에게 풀을 많이 줘야 할까?" "왜 그런 걸 묻지?" "내가 사는 곳은 아주 작거든…." "거기 있는 걸로도 충분할 거야." 내가 말했다. "내가 준 건 아주 작은 양이니까." 그는 고개를 숙여 그림을 들여다보았다. "그렇게 작지도 않은걸. 이거 봐! 잠이 들었어…." 나는 이렇게 어린 왕자를 알게 되었다.

I t took me a long time to learn where he came from. The little prince, who asked me so many questions, never seemed to hear the ones I asked him. It was from words dropped by chance that, little by little, everything was revealed to me.

The first time he saw my airplane, for instance (I shall not draw my airplane; that would be much too complicated for me), he asked me:

"What is that object?"

"That is not an object. It flies. It is an airplane. It is my airplane."

And I was proud to have him learn that I could fly.

He cried out, then:

"What! You dropped down from the sky?"

"Yes," I answered, modestly.

"Oh! That is funny!"

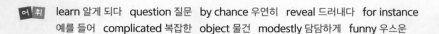

어휘 learn 알게 되다 question 질문 by chance 우연히 reveal 드러내다 for instance 예를 들어 complicated 복잡한 object 물건 modestly 담담하게 funny 우스운

It took me a long time to learn where he came from.

It was from words dropped by chance that, little by little, everything was revealed to me.

"What! You dropped down from the sky?"

 해석

그가 어디서 왔는지 알아내기까지는 오랜 시간이 걸렸다. 어린 왕자는 내게 많은 질문을 던지면서도 내 질문에는 귀를 기울이지 않는 것 같았다. 나는 그가 우연히 내뱉는 말들을 통해 조금씩 모든 것을 알아 가게 되었다. 일례로, 내 비행기를 처음 보았을 때(비행기는 그리지 않을 것이다. 내가 그리기엔 너무 복잡하니까.) 그가 이렇게 물었다. "이 물건은 대체 뭐야?" "이건 물건이 아니라 하늘을 나는 거야. 비행기지. 내 비행기야." 나는 그에게 날 수 있다는 이야기를 하면서 자부심을 느꼈다. 그러자 그가 소리쳤다. "뭐라고? 아저씨가 하늘에서 떨어졌단 말이야?" "맞아." 나는 담담하게 대답했다. "우와, 그것 참 재미있네!"

And the little prince broke into a lovely peal of laughter, which irritated me very much. I like my misfortunes to be taken seriously.

Then he added:

"So you, too, come from the sky! Which is your planet?"

At that moment I caught a gleam of light in the impenetrable mystery of his presence; and I demanded, abruptly:

"Do you come from another planet?"

But he did not reply. He tossed his head gently, without taking his eyes from my plane:

"It is true that on that you can't have come from very far away..."

And he sank into a reverie, which lasted a long time. Then, taking my sheep out of his pocket, he buried himself in the contemplation of his treasure.

 어휘 break into (갑자기) ~하다 peal 큰 소리 laughter 웃음 misfortune 불운 seriously 심각하게 planet 행성 impenetrable 불가해한 reverie 몽상 contemplation 사색

And the little prince broke into a lovely peal of laughter, which irritated me very much.

At that moment I caught a gleam of light in the impenetrable mystery of his presence; and I demanded, abruptly.

"Do you come from another planet?"

그가 즐겁다는 듯 큰 소리로 웃음을 터뜨리자 나는 기분이 매우 나빠졌다. 상대방이 내 불행을 진지하게 받아들여 주길 바랐기 때문이다. 그때 어린 왕자가 덧붙였다. "그럼 아저씨도 하늘에서 온 거네! 어느 별에서 왔어?" 그 순간 문득 그의 신비로운 존재를 이해하는 데 필요한 한 줄기 빛이 비쳤다. 나는 불쑥 질문을 던졌다. "넌 다른 별에서 왔니?" 하지만 그는 대답하지 않았다. 대신 내 비행기 쪽으로 부드럽게 시선을 던졌다. "저런 걸 타고 그렇게 멀리서 오진 못했을 거야…." 그는 한참 동안 깊은 생각에 잠겼다. 그러더니 주머니에서 내가 그려 준 양 그림을 꺼내더니 그 보물을 빤히 응시했다.

You can imagine how my curiosity was aroused by this half-confidence about the "other planets." I made a great effort, therefore, to find out more on this subject.

"My little man, where do you come from? What is this 'where I live,' of which you speak? Where do you want to take your sheep?"

After a reflective silence he answered:

"The thing that is so good about the box you have given me is that at night he can use it as his house."

"That is so. And if you are good I will give you a string, too, so that you can tie him during the day, and a post to tie him to."

But the little prince seemed shocked by this offer:

"Tie him! What a queer idea!"

"But if you don't tie him," I said, "he will wander off somewhere, and get lost."

어휘 curiosity 호기심 arise 생기다 half-confidence 반신반의 reflective 사색적인
silence 침묵 tie 묶다 during ~하는 동안 queer 기묘한, 이상한 wander 헤매다

You can imagine how my curiosity was aroused by this half-confidence about the "other planets."

"Tie him! What a queer idea!"

"But if you don't tie him," I said, "he will wander off somewhere, and get lost."

'다른 별'이라는 표현에 반신반의하며 어떤 호기심을 불러일으켰을지 상상하기란 어렵지 않을 것이다. 나는 그 말에 대해 좀 더 알아내려고 애썼다. "꼬마야, 넌 어디서 왔니? 네가 말하는 '사는 곳'이 어디야? 그 양을 어디로 데려가려는 거지?" 그는 말없이 생각에 잠겨 있다가 입을 열었다. "아저씨가 준 상자가 밤에는 양의 집이 되어줄 테니 참 다행이야." "맞아. 네가 착하게 군다면 밧줄도 줄게. 그걸로 낮 동안에 양을 묶어 둘 수 있을 거야." 하지만 어린 왕자는 내 제안에 충격을 받은 것 같았다. "묶어 둔다고? 정말 이상한 생각이네!" "하지만 묶어 두지 않으면 아무 데나 돌아다니다가 길을 잃어버릴지도 몰라."

My friend broke into another peal of laughter:

"But where do you think he would go?"

"Anywhere. Straight ahead of him."

Then the little prince said, earnestly:

"That doesn't matter. Where I live, everything is so small!"

And, with perhaps a hint of sadness, he added:

"Straight ahead of him, nobody can go very far..."

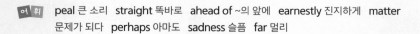

어휘 peal 큰 소리 straight 똑바로 ahead of ~의 앞에 earnestly 진지하게 matter 문제가 되다 perhaps 아마도 sadness 슬픔 far 멀리

"But where do you think he would go?"

_____

_____

"That doesn't matter. Where I live, everything is so small!"

_____

_____

"Straight ahead of him, nobody can go very far..."

_____

_____

내 친구는 또다시 크게 웃음을 터뜨렸다. "돌아다니긴 어딜 돌아다녀?" "어디든. 앞으로 곧장 걸어갈 수 있겠지." 어린 왕자는 진지하게 말했다. "괜찮아. 내가 사는 곳은 모든 것이 아주 작거든!" 그러더니 약간 서글픈 기색으로 덧붙였다. "앞으로 곧장 걸어가도 멀리는 가지 못할 거야…."

I had thus learned a second fact of great importance: this was that the planet the little prince came from was scarcely any larger than a house!

But that did not really surprise me much. I knew very well that in addition to the great planets--such as the Earth, Jupiter, Mars, Venus--to which we have given names, there are also hundreds of others, some of which are so small that one has a hard time seeing them through the telescope. When an astronomer discovers one of these he does not give it a name, but only a number. He might call it, for example, "Asteroid 325."

여휘 second 두 번째 importance 중요성 scarcely 거의 ~하지 않다 through ~를 통해
telescope 망원경 astronomer 천문학자 discover 발견하다 asteroid 소행성

I had thus learned a second fact of great importance.

This was that the planet the little prince came from was scarcely any larger than a house!

When an astronomer discovers one of these he does not give it a name, but only a number.

이렇게 해서 나는 아주 중요한 두 번째 사실을 알게 되었다. 어린 왕자가 사는 별은 집 한 채보다 클까 말까한 정도였다! 하지만 그건 별로 놀랍지 않았다. 나는 우주에 지구, 목성, 화성, 금성처럼 우리가 이름을 붙여 준 거대한 행성뿐만 아니라 수백 개의 다른 별들이, 개중에는 너무 작아서 망원경으로 관찰할 수조차 없는 별들이 존재한다는 사실을 잘 알고 있었다. 천문학자가 그런 별을 발견하면 이름 대신 번호를 붙인다. 이를테면 '소행성 325'라고 명명하는 식이다.

I have serious reason to believe that the planet from which the little prince came is the asteroid known as B-612.

This asteroid has only once been seen through the telescope. That was by a Turkish astronomer, in 1909.

On making his discovery, the astronomer had presented it to the International Astronomical Congress, in a great demonstration. But he was in Turkish costume, and so nobody would believe what he said.

Grown-ups are like that...

Fortunately, however, for the reputation of Asteroid B-612, a Turkish dictator made a law that his subjects, under pain of death, should change to European costume.

어휘 serious 중대한 reason 이유 telescope 망원경 astronomer 천문학자 present 보여주다 demonstration 설명 costume 의상 reputation 명성 dictator 독재자

I have serious reason to believe that the planet from which the little prince came is the asteroid known as B-612.

On making his discovery, the astronomer had presented it to the International Astronomical Congress, in a great demonstration.

But he was in Turkish costume, and so nobody would believe what he said.

So in 1920 the astronomer gave his demonstration all over again, dressed with impressive style and elegance. And this time everybody accepted his report.

If I have told you these details about the asteroid, and made a note of its number for you, it is on account of the grown-ups and their ways. When you tell them that you have made a new friend, they never ask you any questions about essential matters. They never say to you, "What does his voice sound like? What games does he love best? Does he collect butterflies?" Instead, they demand: "How old is he? How many brothers has he? How much does he weigh? How much money does his father make?" Only from these figures do they think they have learned anything about him.

---

 impressive 인상적인   elegance 기품   accept 받아들이다   detail 세부사항
on account of ~때문에   essential 필수적인   weigh 무게가 나가다   figure 숫자, 수치

So in 1920 the astronomer gave his demonstration all over again, dressed with impressive style and elegance.

_____

_____

And this time everybody accepted his report.

_____

_____

"What does his voice sound like? What games does he love best? Does he collect butterflies?"

_____

_____

천문학자는 1920년에 인상적인 스타일에 기품 있는 옷을 차려입고 증명을 다시 한번 해 보였다. 이번에는 모두가 그의 주장을 받아들였다. 내가 소행성 B-612에 대해 번호까지 알려주며 자세히 설명하는 것은 모두 어른들과 그들이 생각하는 방식 때문이다. 만약 어른들에게 새로운 친구를 사귀었다고 말하면, 그들은 절대 진짜 중요한 것에 대해 묻지 않는다. 가령 "그 아이의 목소리는 어떻니? 어떤 놀이를 가장 좋아하니? 그 아이는 나비를 수집하니?" 같은 질문은 결코 들을 수 없다. 그 대신 이렇게 묻는다. "걔는 몇 살이니? 형제는 몇 명이고? 몸무게는 얼마나 나간다니? 그 아이 아버지는 수입이 얼마라든?" 그리고는 필요한 정보를 모두 알았다고 생각하는 것이다.

If you were to say to the grown-ups: "I saw a beautiful house made of rosy brick, with geraniums in the windows and doves on the roof," they would not be able to get any idea of that house at all. You would have to say to them: "I saw a house that cost $20,000." Then they would exclaim: "Oh, what a pretty house that is!"

Just so, you might say to them: "The proof that the little prince existed is that he was charming, that he laughed, and that he was looking for a sheep. If anybody wants a sheep, that is a proof that he exists." And what good would it do to tell them that? They would shrug their shoulders, and treat you like a child. But if you said to them: "The planet he came from is Asteroid B-612," then they would be convinced, and leave you in peace from their questions.

They are like that. One must not hold it against them. Children should always show great forbearance toward grown-up people.

---

 rosy 장밋빛　brick 벽돌　geranium 제라늄 (꽃)　dove 비둘기　exclaim 외치다
proof 증거　exist 존재하다　convince 설득하다　forbearance 관용

"I saw a beautiful house made of rosy brick, with geraniums in the windows and doves on the roof."

"The proof that the little prince existed is that he was charming, that he laughed, and that he was looking for a sheep."

어른들에게 이런 말을 던진다고 생각해 보자. "장밋빛 벽돌로 지은 예쁜 집을 봤어요. 창가에는 제라늄 화분이 있고 지붕에는 비둘기들이 앉아 있었어요." 그들은 그 집이 어떤 집인지 전혀 상상하지 못할 것이다. 반면 이렇게 말했다고 치자. "2만 달러짜리 집을 봤어요." 그러면 그들은 당장 외칠 것이다. "이야, 정말 멋진 집이구나!" 똑같은 이치로, 당신은 어른들에게 이런 설명을 할 수 있다. "어린 왕자가 있었다는 증거는 그가 매혹적이었고, 환하게 웃었고, 양 한 마리를 갖고 싶어 했다는 거예요. 누군가 양을 원한다는 건 바로 그가 존재한다는 증거예요." 하지만 그게 무슨 소용이겠는가? 그들은 어깨를 으쓱하고는 당신을 어린아이 취급할 것이다. 반면 "그는 소행성 B-612에서 왔어요."라고 말한다면, 그들은 당신의 말을 받아들이고 더 이상 귀찮은 질문을 던지지 않을 것이다. 어른들은 그런 식이다. 하지만 그들을 나쁘게 생각해서는 안 된다. 어린이들은 항상 커다란 인내심을 갖고 어른들을 대해야 한다.

But certainly, for us who understand life, figures are a matter of indifference. I should have liked to begin this story in the fashion of the fairy-tales. I should have like to say: "Once upon a time there was a little prince who lived on a planet that was scarcely any bigger than himself, and who had need of a sheep..."

To those who understand life, that would have given a much greater air of truth to my story.

For I do not want any one to read my book carelessly. I have suffered too much grief in setting down these memories. Six years have already passed since my friend went away from me, with his sheep. If I try to describe him here, it is to make sure that I shall not forget him. To forget a friend is sad. Not every one has had a friend. And if I forget him, I may become like the grown-ups who are no longer interested in anything but figures...

---

 certainly 분명히 a matter of indifference 관심 밖의 일 fairy-tale 동화
truth 진실 carelessly 무심하게 grief 슬픔 describe 묘사하다 be interested in
~에 흥미가 있는

But certainly, for us who understand life, figures are a matter of indifference.

If I try to describe him here, it is to make sure that I shall not forget him.

And if I forget him, I may become like the grown-ups who are no longer interested in anything but figures...

하지만 인생이 뭔지 아는 우리에게 숫자는 관심 밖의 일이다. 나는 이 이야기를 동화 같이 시작하고 싶었다. 이런 식으로. "옛날 옛적에 자기 몸보다 클까 말까 한 별에 살던 어린 왕자가 있었답니다. 어린 왕자는 양 한 마리를 가지고 싶었어요…." 인생의 의미를 이해하는 사람들에게는 그 편이 훨씬 진실하게 읽힐 테니까. 하지만 나는 사람들이 이 책을 무성의하게 읽길 바라지 않는다. 내게 이 이야기는 꺼낼 때마다 큰 슬픔이 밀려오는 기억이다. 내 친구가 그의 양과 함께 떠나 버린 뒤로 벌써 6년이 지났다. 이 책에서 그를 열심히 묘사하는 것은 그를 잊지 않기 위해서이다. 친구를 잊는다는 건 슬픈 일이다. 친구는 누구나 가질 수 있는 존재가 아니다. 만약 그를 잊는다면, 나는 숫자 외에 아무런 관심도 없는 어른들처럼 되어 버릴지도 모른다….

It is for that purpose, again, that I have bought a box of paints and some pencils. It is hard to take up drawing again at my age, when I have never made any pictures except those of the boa constrictor from the outside and the boa constrictor from the inside, since I was six. I shall certainly try to make my portraits as true to life as possible. But I am not at all sure of success. One drawing goes along all right, and another has no resemblance to its subject. I make some errors, too, in the little prince's height: in one place he is too tall and in another too short. And I feel some doubts about the color of his costume. So I fumble along as best I can, now good, now bad, and I hope generally fair-to-middling.

In certain more important details I shall make mistakes, also. But that is something that will not be my fault. My friend never explained anything to me. He thought, perhaps, that I was like himself. But I, alas, do not know how to see sheep through the walls of boxes. Perhaps I am a little like the grown-ups. I have had to grow old.

어휘 purpose 목적 except ~을 제외하고 resemblance 닮음 fumble 더듬거리다
fair to middling 좋지도 나쁘지도 않은 fault 잘못 alas 아아(유감을 나타내는 소리)

I shall certainly try to make my portraits as true to life as possible.

He thought, perhaps, that I was like himself.

But I, alas, do not know how to see sheep through the walls of boxes.

내가 물감 한 상자와 연필 몇 자루를 산 것도 이런 이유 때문이다. 여섯 살, 그러니까 속이 보이거나 보이지 않는 보아뱀을 그린 이후로 아무것도 그려 본 적 없는 내가, 이 나이에 다시 그림을 시작한다는 건 쉽지 않은 일이다. 최대한 그의 실물에 가까운 그림들을 보여 주도록 노력하겠지만, 성공할지는 잘 모르겠다. 어떤 그림은 꽤 괜찮지만, 또 어떤 그림은 그와 닮은 구석이 전혀 없다. 때로는 어린 왕자의 키를 잘못 묘사하기도 한다. 여기서는 너무 크고 저기서는 너무 작게 그려진다. 그가 입었던 옷 색깔도 확신할 수 없다. 이런 와중에 더듬거리며 최선을 다해 나아가는 것이다. 때로는 잘 그리고, 때로는 망치고, 그래도 전반적으로는 나쁘지 않기를 바라면서. 아마 그보다 더 중요한 부분들에서도 실수를 저지를 것이다. 하지만 그건 내 잘못이 아니다. 내 친구는 설명해 주는 법이 없었기 때문이다. 그는 내가 자신과 비슷하다고 생각했던 것 같다. 아아, 그러나 불행히도 나는 상자 안에 담긴 양을 볼 줄 모른다. 어쩌면 나 역시 어른들과 조금은 비슷할지도 모르겠다. 너무 나이를 먹어 버린 것이다.

As each day passed I would learn, in our talk, something about the little prince's planet, his departure from it, his journey. The information would come very slowly, as it might chance to fall from his thoughts. It was in this way that I heard, on the third day, about the catastrophe of the baobabs.

This time, once more, I had the sheep to thank for it. For the little prince asked me abruptly--as if seized by a grave doubt-- "It is true, isn't it, that sheep eat little bushes?"

"Yes, that is true."

"Ah! I am glad!"

I did not understand why it was so important that sheep should eat little bushes. But the little prince added:

"Then it follows that they also eat baobabs?"

I pointed out to the little prince that baobabs were not little bushes, but, on the contrary, trees as big as castles; and that even if he took a whole herd of elephants away with him, the herd would not eat up one single baobab.

 pass 지나다 departure 떠남, 출발 catastrophe 재앙 abruptly 갑자기 seize 엄습하다, 몰려오다 grave 심각한 bush 덤불 castle 성, 성곽 herd 떼

As each day passed I would learn, in our talk, something about the little prince's planet, his departure from it, his journey.

I pointed out to the little prince that baobabs were not little bushes, but, on the contrary, trees as big as castles.

하루가 갈수록 나는 어린 왕자의 별과 그가 떠나온 날과 지나온 여정에 대해 조금씩 알아가게 되었다. 그 정보들은 아주 천천히, 그의 생각을 타고 조금씩 흘러나왔다. 그를 만난 지 사흘째 되던 날 바오바브나무의 비극을 알게 된 것도 이런 방식을 통해서였다. 이번에도 역시 양 덕분이었다. 그때 어린 왕자는 심각한 두려움에 사로잡힌 표정으로 불쑥 질문을 던졌다. "양이 작은 덤불을 먹어 치운다는 게 정말이야?" "그럼. 정말이지." "오! 그거 잘됐네!" 나는 양이 작은 덤불을 먹는다는 사실이 어째서 그렇게 중요한지 이해할 수 없었다. 그러나 어린 왕자는 이렇게 덧붙였다. "그럼 바오바브나무 덤불도 먹겠지?" 나는 어린 왕자에게 바오바브나무는 작은 덤불이 아니라 성만큼이나 큰 나무라는 사실을 알려 주었다. 코끼리 떼가 달려들어도 단 한 그루의 바오바브나무조차 먹어 치우지 못하리라는 사실도.

The idea of the herd of elephants made the little prince laugh.

"We would have to put them one on top of the other," he said.

But he made a wise comment:

"Before they grow so big, the baobabs start out by being little."

"That is strictly correct," I said. "But why do you want the sheep to eat the little baobabs?"

He answered me at once, "Oh, come, come!", as if he were speaking of something that was self-evident. And I was obliged to make a great mental effort to solve this problem, without any assistance.

어휘 strictly 정확히 correct 옳은 self-evident 자명한 be obliged to ~을 해야 하다
mental 내면의 assistance 도움

The idea of the herd of elephants made the little prince laugh.

"Before they grow so big, the baobabs start out by being little."

And I was obliged to make a great mental effort to solve this problem, without any assistance.

어린 왕자는 코끼리 떼라는 말을 듣고 웃었다. "코끼리들을 포개 놓아야겠네." 그리고는 매우 총명한 말을 덧붙였다. "하지만 커다랗게 자라기 전에는 바오바브나무도 작은 덤불이잖아." "그건 맞는 말이야." 내가 대답했다. "그런데 어째서 양에게 어린 바오바브나무를 먹이려는 거지?" 그는 망설임 없이 답했다. "아이, 생각해 봐!" 그의 목소리가 너무나 당연하다는 투였으므로, 나는 아무런 힌트도 없이 문제를 풀기 위해 속으로 끙끙 앓아야 했다.

Indeed, as I learned, there were on the planet where the little prince lived--as on all planets--good plants and bad plants. In consequence, there were good seeds from good plants, and bad seeds from bad plants. But seeds are invisible. They sleep deep in the heart of the earth's darkness, until some one among them is seized with the desire to awaken. Then this little seed will stretch itself and begin--timidly at first--to push a charming little sprig inoffensively upward toward the sun. If it is only a sprout of radish or the sprig of a rose bush, one would let it grow wherever it might wish. But when it is a bad plant, one must destroy it as soon as possible, the very first instant that one recognizes it.

어휘   plant 식물   in consequence 결과적으로   seed 씨앗   invisible 보이지 않는   in the heart of ~의 가운데   darkness 어둠   sprig 잔가지   inoffensively 해롭지 않게 sprout 새싹   radish 무   destroy 파괴하다

In consequence, there were good seeds from good plants, and bad seeds from bad plants.

If it is only a sprout of radish or the sprig of a rose-bush, one would let it grow wherever it might wish.

But when it is a bad plant, one must destroy it as soon as possible, the very first instant that one recognizes it.

마침내 나는 어린 왕자가 사는 별에 (다른 모든 별과 마찬가지로) 좋은 식물과 나쁜 식물이 있다는 사실을 알게 되었다. 그 말은 좋은 식물의 좋은 씨앗과 나쁜 식물의 나쁜 씨앗이 있다는 의미였다. 하지만 씨앗들은 눈에 보이지 않는다. 어두컴컴하고 깊은 땅속에 잠들어 있다. 그러다 그중 하나가 문득 깨어나고 싶은 열망에 사로잡힌다. 그러면 그 씨앗은 기지개를 켜며 (처음에는 소심하게) 귀엽고 아무런 해가 없는 작은 가지를 태양이 있는 쪽으로 쏙 내민다. 그것이 무의 새싹이나 장미의 잔가지라면, 그대로 내버려둬도 좋다. 하지만 나쁜 식물의 싹이라면 눈에 띄는 대로 즉시 뽑아 버려야 한다.

5

Now there were some terrible seeds on the planet that was the home of the little prince; and these were the seeds of the baobab. The soil of that planet was infested with them. A baobab is something you will never, never be able to get rid of if you attend to it too late. It spreads over the entire planet. It bores clear through it with its roots. And if the planet is too small, and the baobabs are too many, they split it in pieces...

"It is a question of discipline," the little prince said to me later on. "When you've finished your own toilet in the morning, then it is time to attend to the toilet of your planet, just so, with the greatest care. You must see to it that you pull up regularly all the baobabs, at the very first moment when they can be distinguished from the rosebushes which they resemble so closely in their earliest youth. It is very tedious work," the little prince added, "but very easy."

어휘   infest 들끓다   get rid of 제거하다   attend to ~을 처리하다   root 뿌리   discipline 규율   distinguish 구별하다   resemble 닮다   tedious 따분한

A baobab is something you will never, never be able to get rid of if you attend to it too late.

You must see to it that you pull up regularly all the baobabs, at the very first moment when they can be distinguished from the rosebushes which they resemble so closely in their earliest youth.

그리고 어린 왕자가 살던 별에는 무시무시한 씨앗들이 있었다. 그것은 바로 바오바브나무 씨앗이었다. 그 별의 땅에는 바오바브나무 씨앗이 우글거리고 있었다. 바오바브나무는 한 번 시기를 놓치면 절대로, 무슨 짓을 해도 뿌리 뽑을 수 없는 존재다. 그렇게 되면 나무들이 별 전체로 퍼져 뿌리로 땅에 구멍을 낸다. 그런데 어린 왕자의 별은 너무 작으므로, 바오바브나무가 너무 많아지면 산산이 부서져 버릴 것이다…. "그건 규율의 문제야." 훗날 어린 왕자가 말했다. "아침에 몸단장을 하고 나면 아주 꼼꼼히 공을 들여서 별의 몸단장도 해 줘야 해. 바오바브나무의 어린 새싹은 장미 덤불과 구분하기 어려우니까. 일단 구분할 수 있을 정도로 자라면 즉시 전부 뽑아 버리는 작업을 규칙적으로 해야 해. 꽤 따분한 일이지." 그리고 이렇게 덧붙였다. "하지만 정말 쉬운 일이야."

And one day he said to me: "You ought to make a beautiful drawing, so that the children where you live can see exactly how all this is. That would be very useful to them if they were to travel some day. Sometimes," he added, "there is no harm in putting off a piece of work until another day. But when it is a matter of baobabs, that always means a catastrophe. I knew a planet that was inhabited by a lazy man. He neglected three little bushes..."

So, as the little prince described it to me, I have made a drawing of that planet. I do not much like to take the tone of a moralist. But the danger of the baobabs is so little understood, and such considerable risks would be run by anyone who might get lost on an asteroid, that for once I am breaking through my reserve. "Children," I say plainly, "watch out for the baobabs!"

My friends, like myself, have been skirting this danger for a long time, without ever knowing it; and so it is for them that I have worked so hard over this drawing. The lesson which I pass on by this means is worth all the trouble it has cost me.

어휘 catastrophe 재앙 inhabited 사는, 거주하는 neglect 무시하다 moralist 도덕가
considerable 상당한 reserve 신중함, 내성적인 plainly 분명하게 skirt (가장자리를)
둘러 가다 lesson 교훈

"You ought to make a beautiful drawing, so that the children where you live can see exactly how all this is."

"I knew a planet that was inhabited by a lazy man."

"Children," I say plainly, "watch out for the baobabs!"

하루는 그가 말했다. "지구에 사는 아이들이 그 작업을 정확히 이해할 수 있도록 예쁜 그림을 그려 줘. 그 아이들이 언젠가 여행을 하게 될 때 도움이 되도록 말이야. 때로는 할 일을 다른 날로 미뤄도 별 탈이 없을 때도 있지. 하지만 바오바브나무를 미뤄 뒀다간 재앙이 일어날 거야. 나는 게으름뱅이가 살고 있던 어느 별을 알아. 그는 작은 나무 덤불 세 개를 방치했지…" 그래서 나는 어린 왕자가 묘사해 준 대로 게으름뱅이의 별을 그렸다. 나는 평소에 도덕군자처럼 얘기하는 걸 좋아하지 않는다. 하지만 바오바브나무의 위험성이 너무 과소평가되고 있으며, 그로 인해 소행성에서 길을 잃은 사람이 겪게 될 위험이 너무 크기에 이번 한 번은 침묵을 깨고 분명히 말하려 한다. "어린이들이여, 바오바브나무를 조심하라!" 내 친구들은 나와 마찬가지로 자신도 모르는 사이에 오랜 세월 이런 위험에 노출되어 있었다. 내가 이 그림을 이토록 열심히 그린 것은 그들을 위해서다. 이 그림에 담긴 교훈에는 나의 수고를 보상할 만한 가치가 있다.

Perhaps you will ask me, "Why are there no other drawing in this book as magnificent and impressive as this drawing of the baobabs?"

The reply is simple. I have tried. But with the others I have not been successful. When I made the drawing of the baobabs I was carried beyond myself by the inspiring force of urgent necessity.

어휘 magnificent 멋진 impressive 인상적인 reply 답변 successful 성공적인
carry ~로 데려가다 beyond ~ 너머로 inspiring 영감을 주는 urgent 긴급한

"Why are there no other drawing in this book as magnificent and impressive as this drawing of the baobabs?"

I have tried. But with the others I have not been successful.

When I made the drawing of the baobabs I was carried beyond myself by the inspiring force of urgent necessity.

어쩌면 여러분은 이렇게 물을지도 모른다. "어째서 이 책에는 바오바브나무 그림만큼 멋지고 인상적인 그림이 더 없나요?" 그 대답은 간단하다. 노력했지만 다른 그림들은 이만큼 성공적으로 그려낼 수 없었다. 바오바브나무를 그릴 때만큼은 다급하고 중요한 마음에 내 능력을 뛰어넘는 영감을 받았던 것이다.

Oh, little prince! Bit by bit I came to understand the secrets of your sad little life... For a long time you had found your only entertainment in the quiet pleasure of looking at the sunset. I learned that new detail on the morning of the fourth day, when you said to me:

"I am very fond of sunsets. Come, let us go look at a sunset now."

"But we must wait," I said.

"Wait? For what?"

"For the sunset. We must wait until it is time."

At first you seemed to be very much surprised. And then you laughed to yourself. You said to me:

"I am always thinking that I am at home!"

Just so. Everybody knows that when it is noon in the United States the sun is setting over France.

어휘   bit by bit 하나씩, 서서히   secret 비밀   entertainment 여흥, 오락   pleasure 즐거움 sunset 석양   surprise 놀라게 하다   noon 정오

For a long time you had found your only entertainment in the quiet pleasure of looking at the sunset.

"I am very fond of sunsets. Come, let us go look at a sunset now."

Everybody knows that when it is noon in the United States the sun is setting over France.

아, 어린 왕자여! 나는 그렇게 조금씩 너의 소박하고 쓸쓸한 삶을 알게 되었지…. 오랜 시간 네게는 석양을 감상하는 즐거움이 유일한 오락거리였어. 나는 그 새로운 사실을 나흘째 되는 날 아침에 알게 되었지. 그날 넌 이렇게 말했어. "나는 석양을 아주 좋아해. 자, 석양을 보러 가자." "그럼 기다려야지." 나는 대답했어. "기다리다니? 뭘 말이야?" "석양을 보려면 해가 질 때까지 기다려야 하잖아." 너는 처음에 몹시 놀란 듯 보이더니 웃음을 터뜨리며 말했어. "난 줄곧 내가 우리 별에 있는 줄 알았지 뭐야!" 그렇게 된 것이다. 미국에서 정오일 때 프랑스에서는 해가 진다는 건 누구나 아는 사실이다.

If you could fly to France in one minute, you could go straight into the sunset, right from noon. Unfortunately, France is too far away for that. But on your tiny planet, my little prince, all you need do is move your chair a few steps. You can see the day end and the twilight falling whenever you like...

"One day," you said to me, "I saw the sunset forty-four times!"

And a little later you added:

"You know--one loves the sunset, when one is so sad..."

"Were you so sad, then?" I asked, "on the day of the forty-four sunsets?"

But the little prince made no reply.

---

 straight 곧장 unfortunately 불행히도 far away 멀리 떨어진 tiny 작은
move 옮기다 twilight 황혼 fall (어둠이) 찾아오다

If you could fly to France in one minute, you could go straight into the sunset, right from noon.

You can see the day end and the twilight falling whenever you like...

"Were you so sad, then?" I asked, "on the day of the forty-four sunsets?"

만약 1분 안에 프랑스까지 날아갈 수 있으면 정오에도 석양을 볼 수 있을 것이다. 불행히도 프랑스는 너무 멀리 있다. 그러나 너의, 그러니까 어린 왕자의 작디작은 별에서는 의자를 몇 발짝 옮겨 놓기만 하면 되지. 그러면 원할 때마다 언제나 하루의 끝자락을 물들인 황혼을 볼 수 있었어···. "하루는" 너는 내게 말했어. "해가 지는 모습을 마흔네 번이나 봤어!" 그리고 잠시 후에 덧붙였지. "왜, 그렇잖아. 너무 슬플 땐 석양을 보고 싶어지니까···." "그럼 그날은 무척 슬펐겠네?" 내가 물었어. "하루에 석양을 마흔네 번 본 날 말이야." 어린 왕자는 대답하지 않았다.

O n the fifth day--again, as always, it was thanks to the sheep--the secret of the little prince's life was revealed to me. Abruptly, without anything to lead up to it, and as if the question had been born of long and silent meditation on his problem, he demanded:

"A sheep--if it eats little bushes, does it eat flowers, too?"

"A sheep," I answered, "eats anything it finds in its reach."

"Even flowers that have thorns?"

"Yes, even flowers that have thorns."

"Then the thorns--what use are they?"

I did not know. At that moment I was very busy trying to unscrew a bolt that had got stuck in my engine. I was very much worried, for it was becoming clear to me that the breakdown of my plane was extremely serious. And I had so little drinking-water left that I had to fear for the worst.

"The thorns--what use are they?"

The little prince never let go of a question, once he had asked it.

어휘 reveal 드러나다 abruptly 갑자기 meditation 명상 demand 묻다 bush 덤불
thorn 가시 unscrew 나사를 풀다 breakdown 고장 let go of ~을 포기하다

Abruptly, without anything to lead up to it, and as if the question had been born of long and silent meditation on his problem,

"A sheep--if it eats little bushes, does it eat flowers, too?"

The little prince never let go of a question, once he had asked it.

닷새째 되는 날, 이번에도 양 덕분에 어린 왕자의 새로운 비밀 하나를 알게 되었다. 그가 불쑥, 아무런 전조도 없이, 마치 오랫동안 혼자 곰곰이 고민한 문제인 듯 이런 질문을 던진 것이다. "양은 작은 덤불을 먹으니까 꽃도 먹겠지?" "양은 먹을 수 있는 건 뭐든 먹어 치우지." 내가 대답했다. "가시가 있는 꽃도?" "그럼. 가시가 있는 꽃도 먹을 수 있어." "그럼 가시는 대체 무엇에 쓰는 거야?" 나는 그 답을 몰랐다. 게다가 하필 그 순간 엔진에 꽉 낀 볼트를 푸느라 정신이 없었다. 비행기 고장이 매우 심각한 것으로 드러나기 시작했기 때문에 걱정이 이만저만이 아니었다. 게다가 마실 물이 바닥을 보이고 있었으므로 최악의 상황까지 생각해야 했다. "가시는 무엇에 쓰는 거야?" 어린 왕자는 한 번 질문하면 절대 포기하는 법이 없었다.

As for me, I was upset over that bolt. And I answered with the first thing that came into my head:

"The thorns are of no use at all. Flowers have thorns just for spite!"

"Oh!"

There was a moment of complete silence. Then the little prince flashed back at me, with a kind of resentfulness:

"I don't believe you! Flowers are weak creatures. They are naïve. They reassure themselves as best they can. They believe that their thorns are terrible weapons..."

I did not answer. At that instant I was saying to myself: "If this bolt still won't turn, I am going to knock it out with the hammer." Again the little prince disturbed my thoughts:

"And you actually believe that the flowers--"

"Oh, no!" I cried. "No, no, no! I don't believe anything. I answered you with the first thing that came into my head. Don't you see--I am very busy with matters of consequence!"

어휘 upset over ~에 대해 걱정하다 of no use 쓸모 없는 spite 앙심, 악의 creature 생물
naïve 순진한 weapon 무기 instant 순간 disturb 방해하다

"The thorns are of no use at all. Flowers have thorns just for spite!"

_____

_____

"I don't believe you! Flowers are weak creatures. They are naïve. They reassure themselves as best they can. They believe that their thorns are terrible weapons..."

_____

_____

_____

_____

하지만 나는 볼트 때문에 신경이 곤두서 있었다. 그래서 생각나는 대로 아무렇게나 대답해 버렸다. "가시는 아무짝에도 쓸모가 없어. 꽃들이 괜히 심술을 부리려고 달고 있는 거야." "그래?" 그는 입을 꾹 다물었다가 잠시 후 내가 원망스럽다는 듯 쏘아붙였다. "안 믿어! 꽃들은 연약한 생물이야. 순진하기도 하고. 그들은 그저 안심하고 싶어서 애쓰는 거야. 자신이 달고 있는 가시가 무시무시한 무기라고 믿는 거라고." 나는 대답하지 않았고, 순간 속으로 이런 생각을 하고 있었다. "볼트가 계속 움직이지 않으면 망치로 두들겨서 빼내야겠다." 어린 왕자는 또다시 내 생각을 방해했다. "그런데 아저씨는 정말로 꽃들이⋯." "오, 제발!" 나는 언성을 높여 대답했다. "이제 그만 좀 해! 아무려면 어때. 난 그저 떠오르는 대로 대답했을 뿐이야. 지금 중요한 일을 하느라 바쁜 게 안 보이니?"

He stared at me, thunderstruck.

"Matters of consequence!"

He looked at me there, with my hammer in my hand, my fingers black with engine-grease, bending down over an object which seemed to him extremely ugly.

"You talk just like the grown-ups!"

That made me a little ashamed. But he went on, relentlessly:

"You mix everything up together... You confuse everything..."

He was really very angry. He tossed his golden curls in the breeze.

"I know a planet where there is a certain red-faced gentleman. He has never smelled a flower. He has never looked at a star. He has never loved any one. He has never done anything in his life but add up figures. And all day he says over and over, just like you: 'I am busy with matters of consequence!' And that makes him swell up with pride. But he is not a man--he is a mushroom!"

---

 stare at ~를 바라보다 thunderstruck 벼락을 맞은 듯한 grease 기름 ashamed 부끄러운 relentlessly 가차 없이 toss 흔들리다 curl 곱슬머리 breeze 산들바람

He looked at me there, with my hammer in my hand, my fingers black with engine-grease, bending down over an object which seemed to him extremely ugly.

"You talk just like the grown-ups!"

But he is not a man--he is a mushroom!"

그는 깜짝 놀란 표정으로 나를 보았다. "중요한 일이라고!" 그는 한 손에 망치를 들고, 손가락은 엔진에서 나온 기름으로 검게 물들고, 끔찍하게 흉물스러운 물건 위로 몸을 기울이고 있는 나를 바라보았다. "아저씨는 꼭 어른들처럼 말하네!" 그 말에 나는 조금 부끄러워졌다. 하지만 그는 가차 없이 말을 이었다. "아저씨는 뒤죽박죽이야. 모든 걸 혼동하고 있단 말이야…" 그는 정말로 화가 나 있었다. 그의 금빛 머리칼이 바람에 흩날렸다. "시뻘건 얼굴의 신사가 사는 별을 알고 있어. 그는 살면서 꽃향기를 맡아 본 적이 없었지. 별을 바라본 적도 없고, 누군가를 사랑해 본 적도 없어. 숫자를 계산하는 것 말고는 아무 일도 해 본 적이 없는 거야. 그는 하루 종일 아저씨랑 똑같은 말을 반복해. '나는 중요한 일을 하느라 바빠!' 그 말을 하면서 자부심으로 가득 차 있지. 하지만 그런 건 사람이 아니야. 그건 버섯이야!"

"A what?"

"A mushroom!"

The little prince was now white with rage.

"The flowers have been growing thorns for millions of years. For millions of years the sheep have been eating them just the same. And is it not a matter of consequence to try to understand why the flowers go to so much trouble to grow thorns which are never of any use to them? Is the warfare between the sheep and the flowers not important? Is this not of more consequence than a fat red-faced gentleman's sums? And if I know--I, myself--one flower which is unique in the world, which grows nowhere but on my planet, but which one little sheep can destroy in a single bite some morning, without even noticing what he is doing-- Oh! You think that is not important!"

 rage 분노 grow 기르다 warfare 전쟁 between ~사이의 unique 유일한
nowhere 아무 데도 없는 destroy 파괴하다

"The flowers have been growing thorns for millions of years."

_____

_____

For millions of years the sheep have been eating them just the same.

_____

_____

"Is the warfare between the sheep and the flowers not important?"

_____

_____

"뭐라고?" "버섯이라고!" 어린 왕자의 얼굴은 분노로 하얗게 질려 있었다. "꽃들은 수백만 년 전부터 가시를 만들어 왔어. 양들은 수백만 년 전부터 변함없이 꽃을 먹어 왔지. 그런데도 꽃들이 아무 소용도 없는 가시를 만드느라 그렇게 애를 쓰는 이유를 이해하려는 게 중요한 일이 아니라는 거야? 양과 꽃의 전쟁은 중요하지 않다는 거지? 그 시뻘건 얼굴의 뚱뚱한 신사가 하는 계산보다 덜 중요하다는 거잖아! 세상에서 가장 특별한 꽃이, 다른 어느 곳도 아닌 우리 별에서만 자라는 꽃 한 송이가, 자신이 무슨 짓을 저지르는지도 모르는 새끼 양에게 어느 날 아침 한 입에 먹힐 수도 있다는 사실은 아저씨에게 중요한 일이 아니라는 거지!"

His face turned from white to red as he continued:

"If some one loves a flower, of which just one single blossom grows in all the millions and millions of stars, it is enough to make him happy just to look at the stars. He can say to himself, 'Somewhere, my flower is there...' But if the sheep eats the flower, in one moment all his stars will be darkened... And you think that is not important!"

He could not say anything more. His words were choked by sobbing.

어휘   turn 변하다   continue 계속하다   blossom 꽃   moment 순간   darken 어두워지다
choke 숨이 막히다   sob 흐느끼다

"If some one loves a flower, of which just one single blossom grows in all the millions and millions of stars, it is enough to make him happy just to look at the stars."

"But if the sheep eats the flower, in one moment all his stars will be darkened... And you think that is not important!"

 해석

그는 새빨개진 얼굴로 말을 이었다. "수백 수천만 개의 별들 가운데 존재하는 단 한 송이의 꽃을 사랑하는 사람은 별들을 바라보는 것만으로 행복할 수 있어. '저 어딘가에 내 꽃이 있겠지…'라고 생각하는 거야. 하지만 양이 그 꽃을 먹어 치운다면 모든 별이 한순간에 어두워지지…. 그런데도 아저씨는 그게 중요하지 않다는 거야?" 그는 말을 잇지 못했다. 그의 말들은 흐느낌에 삼켜졌다.

The night had fallen. I had let my tools drop from my hands. Of what moment now was my hammer, my bolt, or thirst, or death? On one star, one planet, my planet, the Earth, there was a little prince to be comforted. I took him in my arms, and rocked him. I said to him:

"The flower that you love is not in danger. I will draw you a muzzle for your sheep. I will draw you a railing to put around your flower. I will--"

I did not know what to say to him. I felt awkward and blundering. I did not know how I could reach him, where I could overtake him and go on hand in hand with him once more.

It is such a secret place, the land of tears.

---

 drop 떨어뜨리다 comfort 위로하다 rock 흔들다 muzzle 입마개 railing 울타리
awkward 어색한 blunder 실수하다 overtake 회복하다 hand in hand 친밀한

Of what moment now was my hammer, my bolt, or thirst, or death?

_____

_____

I did not know how I could reach him, where I could overtake him and go on hand in hand with him once more.

_____

_____

It is such a secret place, the land of tears.

_____

_____

밤이 찾아왔다. 나는 들고 있던 연장을 내려놓았다. 지금 이 순간 내게 망치나 볼트 혹은 갈증이나 죽음이 무슨 의미일까? 어떤 별, 어떤 행성 위에, 나의 별인 이 지구 위에, 위로해 주어야 할 어린 왕자가 있다. 나는 그를 두 팔로 감싸고 부드럽게 어르면서 말했다. "네가 사랑하는 꽃은 위험하지 않아. 내가 양에게 채울 입마개를 그려 줄게. 꽃의 주위에 둘러칠 울타리도 그려 줄게. 또…." 나는 무슨 말을 해야 할지 알 수 없었다. 어색하고 서투른 기분이 들었다. 어떻게 그의 마음을 움직이고, 어떻게 그와의 우정을 다시 회복할 수 있을 것인가. 눈물의 나라는 그토록 신비한 세계였다.

I soon learned to know this flower better. On the little prince's planet the flowers had always been very simple. They had only one ring of petals; they took up no room at all; they were a trouble to nobody. One morning they would appear in the grass, and by night they would have faded peacefully away. But one day, from a seed blown from no one knew where, a new flower had come up; and the little prince had watched very closely over this small sprout which was not like any other small sprouts on his planet. It might, you see, have been a new kind of baobab.

어휘 soon 곧 petal 꽃잎 take up (공간을) 차지하다 room 공간 appear 나타나다
grass 잔디 fade 사라지다 peacefully 조용하게

On the little prince's planet the flowers had always been very simple.

But one day, from a seed blown from no one knew where, a new flower had come up; and the little prince had watched very closely over this small sprout which was not like any other small sprouts on his planet.

나는 그 꽃에 대해 더 잘 알게 되었다. 어린 왕자의 별에는 본래 꽃잎이 한 겹으로 난 소박한 꽃들만 자랐다. 그들은 자리를 거의 차지하지 않았고, 누구도 귀찮게 굴지 않았다. 그저 어느 날 아침 풀밭에 나타났다가 저녁이 되면 조용히 사라졌다. 그런데 하루는 어딘지 모를 곳에서 날아온 씨앗 하나가 새로운 꽃을 피웠다. 어린 왕자는 별에서 자라던 다른 어떤 새싹과도 다른 그 새싹을 주의 깊게 관찰했다. 그것은 어쩌면 새로운 종류의 바오바브나무일지도 몰랐다.

The shrub soon stopped growing, and began to get ready to produce a flower. The little prince, who was present at the first appearance of a huge bud, felt at once that some sort of miraculous apparition must emerge from it. But the flower was not satisfied to complete the preparations for her beauty in the shelter of her green chamber. She chose her colors with the greatest care. She dressed herself slowly. She adjusted her petals one by one. She did not wish to go out into the world all rumpled, like the field poppies. It was only in the full radiance of her beauty that she wished to appear. Oh, yes! She was a coquettish creature! And her mysterious adornment lasted for days and days.

Then one morning, exactly at sunrise, she suddenly showed herself.

어휘 shrub 작은 가지 bud 봉오리 apparition 불가사의한 현상 emerge 나타나다
adjust 조정하다 rumple 헝클다 poppy 양귀비 coquettish 요염한
adornment 꾸미기

The little prince, who was present at the first appearance of a huge bud, felt at once that some sort of miraculous apparition must emerge from it.

Then one morning, exactly at sunrise, she suddenly showed herself.

 해석

그러나 그 작은 가지는 이내 성장을 멈추고 꽃을 피울 준비를 시작했다. 커다란 꽃봉오리를 처음 본 순간, 어린 왕자는 그곳에서 뭔가 기적적인 존재가 출현하리라는 예감을 받았다. 하지만 꽃은 그 초록색 공간 안에서 끝없이 아름다워질 준비를 계속할 뿐이었다. 그는 아름다운 빛깔을 세심하게 고르고, 시간을 들여 몸을 단장하고, 꽃잎을 한 장 한 장 다듬었다. 양귀비꽃처럼 흐트러진 모습으로 세상에 나오고 싶지 않았던 것이다. 자신의 아름다움에 물이 한창 올랐을 때, 꽃은 그때 세상에 나타나고 싶었다. 아, 그렇다! 꽃은 요염한 생물이었다! 꽃의 신비로운 몸단장은 그렇게 며칠이고 계속되었다. 어느 날 아침, 해가 떠오르는 바로 그 시간에, 꽃은 갑자기 모습을 드러냈다.

And, after working with all this painstaking precision, she yawned and said:

"Ah! I am scarcely awake. I beg that you will excuse me. My petals are still all disarranged..."

But the little prince could not restrain his admiration:

"Oh! How beautiful you are!"

"Am I not?" the flower responded, sweetly. "And I was born at the same moment as the sun..."

The little prince could guess easily enough that she was not any too modest--but how moving--and exciting--she was!

"I think it is time for breakfast," she added an instant later. "If you would have the kindness to think of my needs--"

And the little prince, completely abashed, went to look for a sprinkling-can of fresh water. So, he tended the flower.

어휘 painstaking 수고를 아끼지 않은 precision 신중함 yawn 하품하다 disarrange 어수선하게 하다 admiration 감탄, 경탄 modest 겸손한 abashed 당황한 sprinkling-can 물뿌리개 tend 돌보다

And, after working with all this painstaking precision, she yawned and said:

"I am scarcely awake. I beg that you will excuse me. My petals are still all disarranged..."

The little prince could guess easily enough that she was not any too modest--but how moving--and exciting--she was!

그런데 그토록 공들여 치장해 놓고, 꽃은 하품을 하며 말했다. "아! 겨우 잠에서 깼답니다. 죄송해요. 꽃잎이 온통 헝클어져 있지요…" 하지만 어린 왕자는 감탄을 억누를 수 없었다. "세상에! 당신은 정말 아름답군요!" "그렇죠?" 꽃이 상냥하게 대답했다. "그리고 저는 태양과 꼭 같은 시간에 태어났답니다…" 어린 왕자는 꽃이 그다지 겸손하지 않은 성격임을 바로 알아챘다. 하지만 그녀는 너무나 흥미롭고 마음을 설레게 하는 존재였다! "아침 식사를 할 시간이군요." 꽃은 이렇게 말하더니 잠시 후 덧붙였다. "친절을 베풀어 제게도 먹을 것을 좀 주시겠어요?" 어린 왕자는 크게 당황한 채로 맑은 물이 담긴 물뿌리개를 찾으러 갔다. 그는 그렇게 꽃을 돌보게 되었다.

So, too, she began very quickly to torment him with her vanity--which was, if the truth be known, a little difficult to deal with. One day, for instance, when she was speaking of her four thorns, she said to the little prince:

"Let the tigers come with their claws!"

"There are no tigers on my planet," the little prince objected. "And, anyway, tigers do not eat weeds."

  torment 괴롭히다 vanity 허영심 speak of ~에 대해 말하다 thorn 가시 claw 발톱
object 이의를 제기하다 weed 풀, 잡초

So, too, she began very quickly to torment him with her vanity--
which was, if the truth be known, a little difficult to deal with.

"Let the tigers come with their claws!"

"There are no tigers on my planet," the little prince objected.

꽃은 태어나자마자 허영심으로 어린 왕자를 괴롭혔다. 솔직히 말해서, 그의 허영은 조금 감당하기 어려운 수준이었다. 예를 들어, 하루는 자신이 가진 네 개의 가시를 두고 어린 왕자에게 말했다. "호랑이들이 발톱을 세우고 달려들어도 괜찮아요!" "이 별에는 호랑이가 없어요." 어린 왕자가 이의를 제기했다. "호랑이는 풀을 먹지도 않고요."

"I am not a weed," the flower replied, sweetly.

"Please excuse me..."

"I am not at all afraid of tigers," she went on, "but I have a horror of drafts. I suppose you wouldn't have a screen for me?"

"A horror of drafts--that is bad luck, for a plant," remarked the little prince, and added to himself, "This flower is a very complex creature..."

"At night I want you to put me under a glass globe. It is very cold where you live. In the place I came from--"

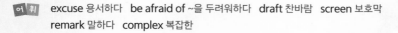

어휘 excuse 용서하다 be afraid of ~을 두려워하다 draft 찬바람 screen 보호막
remark 말하다 complex 복잡한

"I am not a weed," the flower replied, sweetly.

_____

_____

"I am not at all afraid of tigers," she went on, "but I have a horror of drafts. I suppose you wouldn't have a screen for me?"

_____

_____

_____

"This flower is a very complex creature..."

_____

_____

But she interrupted herself at that point. She had come in the form of a seed. She could not have known anything of any other worlds. Embarrassed over having let herself be caught on the verge of such a naïve untruth, she coughed two or three times, in order to put the little prince in the wrong.

"The screen?"

"I was just going to look for it when you spoke to me..."

Then she forced her cough a little more so that he should suffer from remorse just the same.

So the little prince, in spite of all the good will that was inseparable from his love, had soon come to doubt her. He had taken seriously words which were without importance, and it made him very unhappy.

어휘 interrupt 중단하다 form 형태 seed 씨앗 embarrassed 당황한 on the verge of ~의 직전에 cough 기침하다 remorse 후회 inseparable 떼어낼 수 없는

Embarrassed over having let herself be caught on the verge of such a naïve untruth, she coughed two or three times, in order to put the little prince in the wrong.

He had taken seriously words which were without importance, and it made him very unhappy.

꽃은 여기서 입을 다물었다. 그 꽃은 씨앗의 형태로 이 별에 왔다. 이곳 말고는 다른 세상에 대해 아는 것이 없었다. 그토록 빤한 거짓말을 하려다가 들켰다는 사실에 부끄러워진 꽃은 어린 왕자에게 책임을 떠넘기려 연거푸 기침을 했다. "바람막이는요?" "막 찾으러 가려고 했는데 당신이 계속 말을 걸었잖아요…" 그러자 꽃은 어린 왕자가 가책을 느끼게 하려고 가짜 기침을 했다. 어린 왕자는 사랑에서 우러나온 좋은 마음을 가지고 있었음에도 장미를 의심하기 시작했다. 그는 중요하지 않은 말들을 심각하게 받아들였고, 그 결과 매우 불행해졌다.

"I ought not to have listened to her," he confided to me one day. "One never ought to listen to the flowers. One should simply look at them and breathe their fragrance. Mine perfumed all my planet. But I did not know how to take pleasure in all her grace. This tale of claws, which disturbed me so much, should only have filled my heart with tenderness and pity."

And he continued his confidences:

"The fact is that I did not know how to understand anything! I ought to have judged by deeds and not by words. She cast her fragrance and her radiance over me. I ought never to have run away from her... I ought to have guessed all the affection that lay behind her poor little stratagems. Flowers are so inconsistent! But I was too young to know how to love her..."

어휘 ought to ~해야 하다 confide 털어놓다 fragrance 향기 tenderness 다정함 pity 동정심 deed 행동 radiance 빛 stratagem 계획, 술수

"But I did not know how to take pleasure in all her grace."

"I ought to have judged by deeds and not by words."

"But I was too young to know how to love her..."

"꽃의 말에 귀를 기울이지 말았어야 해." 어느 날 그가 내게 말했다. "꽃의 말은 듣지 말아야 했어. 그저 바라보고 향기를 맡아야 했는데. 내 꽃은 온 별을 향기로 물들였어. 그런데도 난 그녀의 우아한 향기를 즐길 줄 몰랐지. 나는 발톱 이야기에 짜증을 냈지만, 사실은 가엾게 여기고 다정하게 대해 줬어야 했어." 그는 계속해서 마음속에 있던 말을 털어놓았다. "그때 난 아무것도 이해할 줄 몰랐어! 그녀의 말이 아니라 행동을 보고 판단했어야 했는데. 그녀는 내게 향기를 선물했고 나를 환하게 밝혀 주었어. 도망쳐선 안 되는 거였는데…. 그 어설픈 계획 뒤에 숨어 있는 애정을 눈치챘어야 했어. 꽃들은 정말 모순된 존재거든! 하지만 꽃을 사랑하기에 그때 난 너무 어렸어…."

I believe that for his escape he took advantage of the migration of a flock of wild birds. On the morning of his departure he put his planet in perfect order. He carefully cleaned out his active volcanoes. He possessed two active volcanoes; and they were very convenient for heating his breakfast in the morning.

He also had one volcano that was extinct. But, as he said, "One never knows!" So he cleaned out the extinct volcano, too. If they are well cleaned out, volcanoes burn slowly and steadily, without any eruptions. Volcanic eruptions are like fires in a chimney. On our earth we are obviously much too small to clean out our volcanoes. That is why they bring no end of trouble upon us.

어휘 escape 빠져나오다 migration (철새의) 이동 departure 출발 active volcano 활화산
possess 가지다 convenient 편리한 extinct 활동을 멈춘 eruption 분출, 폭발
chimney 굴뚝

I believe that for his escape he took advantage of the migration of a flock of wild birds.

On the morning of his departure he put his planet in perfect order.

On our earth we are obviously much too small to clean out our volcanoes.

나는 어린 왕자가 철새들의 이동을 이용해서 자기 별을 떠나왔으리라고 짐작한다. 떠나던 날 아침, 그는 별을 일사불란하게 정리했다. 우선 활화산들을 주의 깊게 청소했다. 그는 두 개의 활화산을 가지고 있었는데, 그것들은 아침밥을 데울 때 아주 유용했다. 그의 별에는 불이 꺼진 사화산도 하나 있었다. 하지만 그의 말마따나 '어떻게 될지는 아무도 모르는 일'이었다. 그는 사화산도 깨끗이 청소했다. 잘 청소된 화산은 폭발하는 일 없이 천천히 규칙적으로 타오른다. 화산 폭발은 굴뚝에서 불이 나는 원리와 비슷하다. 물론 지구에 있는 화산을 청소하기에 우리 인간은 너무나 작다. 이것이 바로 우리가 화산 때문에 끝없이 문제를 겪는 이유다.

The little prince also pulled up, with a certain sense of dejection, the last little shoots of the baobabs. He believed that he would never want to return. But on this last morning all these familiar tasks seemed very precious to him. And when he watered the flower for the last time, and prepared to place her under the shelter of her glass globe, he realized that he was very close to tears.

"Goodbye," he said to the flower.

But she made no answer.

어휘 pull up 뽑다 dejection 우울함 return 돌아오다 familiar 친숙한 precious 소중한
prepare 준비하다 shelter 은신처 realize 깨닫다

The little prince also pulled up, with a certain sense of dejection, the last little shoots of the baobabs.

But on this last morning all these familiar tasks seemed very precious to him.

He realized that he was very close to tears.

어린 왕자는 다소 울적한 기분으로 지금 막 돋아난 바오바브나무의 새싹을 뽑았다. 그는 다시 돌아오려는 마음이 들지 않을 수도 있으리라 생각했다. 그런데 마지막 날 아침에는 익숙했던 모든 일들이 새삼 소중하게 느껴졌다. 꽃에 마지막으로 물을 주고 유리 덮개를 씌워 주려던 순간, 그는 거의 울고 싶은 심정이 되었다. "잘 있어요." 그가 꽃에게 말했다. 하지만 꽃은 대답하지 않았다.

"Goodbye," he said again.

The flower coughed. But it was not because she had a cold.

"I have been silly," she said to him, at last. "I ask your forgiveness. Try to be happy..."

He was surprised by this absence of reproaches. He stood there all bewildered, the glass globe held arrested in mid-air. He did not understand this quiet sweetness.

"Of course I love you," the flower said to him. "It is my fault that you have not known it all the while. That is of no importance. But you--you have been just as foolish as I. Try to be happy... Let the glass globe be. I don't want it any more."

"But the wind--"

"My cold is not so bad as all that... The cool night air will do me good. I am a flower."

"But the animals--"

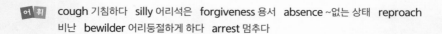

어휘   cough 기침하다   silly 어리석은   forgiveness 용서   absence ~없는 상태   reproach 비난   bewilder 어리둥절하게 하다   arrest 멈추다

"I have been silly," she said to him, at last. "I ask your forgiveness. Try to be happy…"

He was surprised by this absence of reproaches.

He stood there all bewildered, the glass globe held arrested in mid-air.

"잘 있어요." 그가 다시 한 번 말했다. 꽃은 기침을 했다. 하지만 감기 때문은 아니었다. "내가 어리석었어요." 꽃이 마침내 입을 열었다. "날 용서해 줘요. 부디 행복하세요…." 어린 왕자는 비난하지 않는 꽃의 반응에 놀랐다. 그는 당황하여 유리 덮개를 공중에 든 채로 서 있었다. 꽃의 그 차분하고 상냥한 태도가 이해되지 않았다. "내가 당신을 사랑하는 게 당연하잖아요." 꽃이 말했다. "당신이 내 마음을 눈치채지 못한 건 내 잘못이에요. 이제 그런 건 중요하지 않아요. 하지만 당신도 나만큼 바보였어요. 부디 행복하세요…. 유리 덮개는 그냥 두세요. 이제 그런 건 필요 없어요." "하지만 바람이…." "내 감기는 그렇게 심하지 않아요…. 서늘한 밤공기는 내게 좋을 거예요. 난 꽃이잖아요." "하지만 짐승들이…."

"Well, I must endure the presence of two or three caterpillars if I wish to become acquainted with the butterflies. It seems that they are very beautiful. And if not the butterflies--and the caterpillars--who will call upon me? You will be far away... As for the large animals--I am not at all afraid of any of them. I have my claws."

And, naïvely, she showed her four thorns. Then she added:

"Don't linger like this. You have decided to go away. Now go!"

For she did not want him to see her crying. She was such a proud flower...

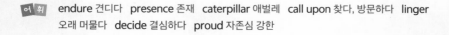

어휘   endure 견디다 presence 존재 caterpillar 애벌레 call upon 찾다, 방문하다 linger 오래 머물다 decide 결심하다 proud 자존심 강한

"Well, I must endure the presence of two or three caterpillars if I wish to become acquainted with the butterflies."

And, naïvely, she showed her four thorns.

For she did not want him to see her crying.

"글쎄요. 나비와 만나려면 애벌레 두세 마리쯤은 견뎌야겠죠. 나비는 정말 아름다운 것 같더군요. 나비나 애벌레가 아니라면 누가 나를 찾아 주겠어요? 당신은 멀리 가 버릴 텐데···. 큰 짐승들은 두렵지 않아요. 내게는 발톱이 있으니까요." 그녀는 순진한 태도로 자신의 가시 네 개를 보여주더니 이렇게 말했다. "그렇게 꾸물거리지 말아요. 이미 떠나기로 결심했잖아요. 그럼 가세요!" 꽃은 울고 있는 자신의 모습을 보이고 싶지 않았다. 그토록 자존심 강한 생물이었던 것이다···.

He found himself in the neighborhood of the asteroids 325, 326, 327, 328, 329, and 330. He began, therefore, by visiting them, in order to add to his knowledge.

The first of them was inhabited by a king. Clad in royal purple and ermine, he was seated upon a throne which was at the same time both simple and majestic.

"Ah! Here is a subject," exclaimed the king, when he saw the little prince coming.

어휘 asteroid 소행성 begin 시작하다 knowledge 지식 inhabit 거주하다 clad ~로 덮인 ermine 담비 throne 왕좌 majestic 위풍당당한

He began, therefore, by visiting them, in order to add to his knowledge.

The first of them was inhabited by a king.

Clad in royal purple and ermine, he was seated upon a throne which was at the same time both simple and majestic.

어린 왕자의 별은 소행성 325, 326, 327, 328, 329, 330과 이웃해 있었다. 그는 지식을 넓힐 겸 일단 이웃 별들을 방문하기로 했다. 첫 번째 별에는 왕이 살고 있었다. 왕은 호화로운 보랏빛 천과 흰 족제비 모피를 휘감은 채 심플하면서도 위엄 있는 왕좌에 앉아 있었다. "오! 여기 신하가 오는군." 어린 왕자가 오는 것을 발견한 왕이 외쳤다.

And the little prince asked himself:

"How could he recognize me when he had never seen me before?"

He did not know how the world is simplified for kings. To them, all men are subjects.

"Approach, so that I may see you better," said the king, who felt consumingly proud of being at last a king over somebody.

The little prince looked everywhere to find a place to sit down; but the entire planet was crammed and obstructed by the king's magnificent ermine robe. So he remained standing upright, and, since he was tired, he yawned.

"It is contrary to etiquette to yawn in the presence of a king," the monarch said to him. "I forbid you to do so."

"I can't help it. I can't stop myself," replied the little prince, thoroughly embarrassed. "I have come on a long journey, and I have had no sleep…"

---

 simplify 단순화하다 subject 신하 approach 접근하다 consumingly 열렬하게
crammed 가득 찬 obstructed 차단된 robe 가운, 예복 upright 똑바로
monarch 군주 thoroughly 완전히 journey 여정

"How could he recognize me when he had never seen me before?"

He did not know how the world is simplified for kings.

The entire planet was crammed and obstructed by the king's magnificent ermine robe.

어린 왕자는 생각했다. "그는 나를 본 적이 없는데 어떻게 내가 신하인 줄 알지?" 왕에게는 세상이 아주 단순하다는 사실을 그는 모르고 있었다. 왕의 눈에는 모든 사람이 자신의 신하이다. "이리 가까이 오라. 짐이 더 잘 볼 수 있도록." 비로소 누군가의 왕 노릇을 하게 되어 매우 뿌듯해진 왕이 말했다. 어린 왕자는 앉을 곳을 찾아 사방을 둘러보았다. 하지만 그 별은 온통 왕의 어마어마한 모피 망토로 뒤덮여 있었다. 그는 할 수 없이 서 있었고, 피곤함에 하품을 했다. "왕 앞에서 하품을 하는 것은 예의에 어긋나느니라." 왕이 말했다. "하품을 금지한다." "어쩔 수 없어요. 참을 수가 없는걸요." 당황한 어린 왕자가 말했다. "저는 먼 길을 여행해 왔고, 내내 잠을 자지 못했거든요…."

"Ah, then," the king said. "I order you to yawn. It is years since I have seen anyone yawning. Yawns, to me, are objects of curiosity. Come, now! Yawn again! It is an order."

"That frightens me... I cannot, any more..." murmured the little prince, now completely abashed.

"Hum! Hum!" replied the king. "Then I--I order you sometimes to yawn and sometimes to--"

He sputtered a little, and seemed vexed.

For what the king fundamentally insisted upon was that his authority should be respected. He tolerated no disobedience. He was an absolute monarch. But, because he was a very good man, he made his orders reasonable.

"If I ordered a general," he would say, by way of example, "if I ordered a general to change himself into a sea bird, and if the general did not obey me, that would not be the fault of the general. It would be my fault."

"May I sit down?" came now a timid inquiry from the little prince.

어휘 order 명령하다 curiosity 호기심 frighten 겁주다 murmur 웅얼거리다 sputter 씩씩거리다 vexed 곤란해하는 insist upon ~을 요구하다 disobedience 불복종

"I order you to yawn. It is years since I have seen anyone yawning."

For what the king fundamentally insisted upon was that his authority should be respected.

Because he was a very good man, he made his orders reasonable.

"그렇다면" 왕이 말했다. "네게 하품을 하도록 명하노라. 지난 몇 년간 하품하는 사람을 보지 못했다. 내게는 하품이 흥미로운 구경거리니라. 자, 어서! 하품을 다시 하라! 명령이다." "그렇게 말씀하시니 무서워서… 하품이 나오지 않아요…." 창피해진 어린 왕자가 웅얼거렸다. "흠! 흠!" 왕이 대답했다. "그렇다면 그대에게 명하노니, 어떤 때는 하품을 하고 어떤 때는…." 그는 씩씩거리고 있었다. 언짢은 기색이었다. 그도 그럴 것이, 왕이 가장 바라는 것은 권위에 대한 존중이었다. 그는 불복종을 용서할 수 없었다. 절대 군주였기 때문이다. 그러나 왕은 동시에 매우 선량한 사람이었기에 명령을 현실적으로 조정했다. 그는 비유를 들어 설명하곤 했다. "만약 짐이 어떤 장군에게 바닷새로 변신하라고 명령했는데 그가 명을 따르지 않는다면, 그건 그의 잘못이 아니니라. 짐의 잘못이지." "좀 앉아도 될까요?" 어린 왕자가 소심하게 물었다.

"I order you to do so," the king answered him, and majestically gathered in a fold of his ermine mantle.

But the little prince was wondering... The planet was tiny. Over what could this king really rule?

"Sire," he said to him, "I beg that you will excuse my asking you a question--"

"I order you to ask me a question," the king hastened to assure him.

"Sire--over what do you rule?"

"Over everything," said the king, with magnificent simplicity.

"Over everything?"

The king made a gesture, which took in his planet, the other planets, and all the stars.

"Over all that?" asked the little prince.

"Over all that," the king answered.

For his rule was not only absolute: it was also universal.

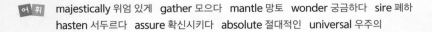

어휘 majestically 위엄 있게 gather 모으다 mantle 망토 wonder 궁금하다 sire 폐하
hasten 서두르다 assure 확신시키다 absolute 절대적인 universal 우주의

"Sire--over what do you rule?"

The king made a gesture, which took in his planet, the other planets, and all the stars.

For his rule was not only absolute: it was also universal.

"그렇게 하라고 명하노라." 왕이 족제비 모피로 된 망토 자락을 위엄 있게 들어 올리며 말했다. 하지만 어린 왕자는 의아했다. 저 왕은 이 작은 별에서 대체 뭘 다스린다는 거지? "폐하." 그가 말했다. "하나만 여쭤봐도 괜찮을까요?" "내게 질문을 하라고 명한다." 왕이 급하게 대답했다. "폐하께서는… 어떤 것을 다스리고 계신가요?" "모든 것을 다스린다." 왕의 대답은 분명하고 당당했다. "모든 것이요?" 왕은 몸짓으로 자신의 별과 다른 별, 우주의 모든 별을 가리켰다. "이 모든 걸 전부요?" 어린 왕자가 물었다. "이 모든 걸 전부 다스리지." 왕이 대답했다. 그는 절대 군주인 동시에 온 우주의 통치자였던 것이다.

"And the stars obey you?"

"Certainly they do," the king said. "They obey instantly. I do not permit insubordination."

Such power was a thing for the little prince to marvel at. If he had been master of such complete authority, he would have been able to watch the sunset, not forty-four times in one day, but seventy-two, or even a hundred, or even two hundred times, without ever having to move his chair. And because he felt a bit sad as he remembered his little planet which he had forsaken, he plucked up his courage to ask the king a favor:

"I should like to see a sunset... Do me that kindness... Order the sun to set..."

"If I ordered a general to fly from one flower to another like a butterfly, or to write a tragic drama, or to change himself into a sea bird, and if the general did not carry out the order that he had received, which one of us would be in the wrong?" the king demanded. "The general, or myself?"

---

 obey 복종하다 permit 허락하다 insubordination 반항 marvel 놀라다 forsake 저버리다 pluck up 용기를 내다 general 장군 tragic 비극의

If he had been master of such complete authority, he would have been able to watch the sunset, not forty-four times in one day, but seventy-two, or even a hundred, or even two hundred times, without ever having to move his chair.

"I should like to see a sunset... Do me that kindness... Order the sun to set..."

"You," said the little prince firmly.

"Exactly. One must require from each one the duty which each one can perform," the king went on. "Accepted authority rests first of all on reason. If you ordered your people to go and throw themselves into the sea, they would rise up in revolution. I have the right to require obedience because my orders are reasonable."

"Then my sunset?" the little prince reminded him: for he never forgot a question once he had asked it.

"You shall have your sunset. I shall command it. But, according to my science of government, I shall wait until conditions are favorable."

"When will that be?" inquired the little prince.

"Hum! Hum!" replied the king; and before saying anything else he consulted a bulky almanac. "Hum! Hum! That will be about--about--that will be this evening about twenty minutes to eight. And you will see how well I am obeyed!"

어휘 firmly 단호히 require 요구하다 duty 의무 revolution 혁명 obedience 복종
reasonable 사리에 맞는 command 명령하다 favorable 알맞은 inquire 질문하다

"One must require from each one the duty which each one can perform,"

"Then my sunset?" the little prince reminded him: for he never forgot a question once he had asked it.

"And you will see how well I am obeyed!"

"폐하께서 잘못하신 거죠." 어린 왕자가 단호하게 대답했다. "맞다. 누구에게든 그가 따를 수 있는 의무를 요구해야 하는 것이니라." 왕은 말을 이어갔다. "권위는 다른 무엇보다도 사리에 근거를 두어야 하느니라. 만약 네가 백성들에게 바다에 몸을 던지라 명령한다면 그들은 혁명을 일으킬 것이다. 내가 복종을 요구할 권리를 가진 것은 내 명령이 사리에 맞기 때문이다." "그럼 제 석양은요?" 한 번 던진 질문은 절대 잊지 않는 어린 왕자가 상기시켰다. "너는 석양을 보게 될 것이다. 내가 그렇게 명령할 테니. 다만 내 통치의 원칙에 따라 조건이 갖춰질 때까지 기다려야 한다." "그게 언제인데요?" 어린 왕자가 물었다. "흠! 흠!" 왕이 커다란 달력을 뒤적이더니 대답했다. "흠! 해는… 오늘 저녁 일곱 시 사십 분 무렵에 질 것이다. 그때가 되면 내 명령이 얼마나 잘 이루어지는지 확인하게 될 것이니라!"

The little prince yawned. He was regretting his lost sunset. And then, too, he was already beginning to be a little bored.

"I have nothing more to do here," he said to the king. "So I shall set out on my way again."

"Do not go," said the king, who was very proud of having a subject. "Do not go. I will make you a Minister!"

"Minister of what?"

"Minster of--of Justice!"

"But there is nobody here to judge!"

"We do not know that," the king said to him. "I have not yet made a complete tour of my kingdom. I am very old. There is no room here for a carriage. And it tires me to walk."

"Oh, but I have looked already!" said the little prince, turning around to give one more glance to the other side of the planet. On that side, as on this, there was nobody at all...

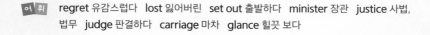

어휘 regret 유감스럽다 lost 잃어버린 set out 출발하다 minister 장관 justice 사법, 법무 judge 판결하다 carriage 마차 glance 힐끗 보다

He was regretting his lost sunset.

"I have nothing more to do here," he said to the king. "So I shall set out on my way again."

"Do not go," said the king, who was very proud of having a subject.

어린 왕자는 하품을 했다. 석양을 볼 수 없다는 사실이 유감스러웠다. 게다가 그는 슬슬 지루해지고 있었다. "이 별에서는 더 할 일이 없는 것 같아요." 그가 왕에게 말했다. "다시 떠나야 할 것 같습니다." "떠나지 말라." 신하를 두게 되어 몹시 뿌듯했던 왕이 말했다. "가지 말아라. 너를 장관으로 임명하겠다!" "무슨 장관인데요?" "음… 법무 장관이니라!" "하지만 여긴 재판할 사람이 아무도 없는걸요!" "그건 모르는 일이다." 왕이 대답했다. "아직 내 왕국을 완전히 조사하지 못했느니라. 짐은 너무 늙었다. 그런데 이 별에는 마차를 둘 자리고 없고 걷기는 힘이 드는구나." "아, 제가 벌써 다 봤어요!" 몸을 돌려 별의 반대쪽 끝을 다시 확인한 어린 왕자가 말했다. 이쪽과 마찬가지로 저쪽에도 사람은 전혀 보이지 않았다.

"Then you shall judge yourself," the king answered. "that is the most difficult thing of all. It is much more difficult to judge oneself than to judge others. If you succeed in judging yourself rightly, then you are indeed a man of true wisdom."

"Yes," said the little prince, "but I can judge myself anywhere. I do not need to live on this planet."

"Hum! Hum!" said the king. "I have good reason to believe that somewhere on my planet there is an old rat. I hear him at night. You can judge this old rat. From time to time you will condemn him to death. Thus his life will depend on your justice. But you will pardon him on each occasion; for he must be treated thriftily. He is the only one we have."

"I," replied the little prince, "do not like to condemn anyone to death. And now I think I will go on my way."

"No," said the king.

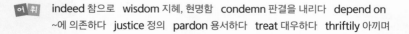

어휘   indeed 참으로   wisdom 지혜, 현명함   condemn 판결을 내리다   depend on
~에 의존하다   justice 정의   pardon 용서하다   treat 대우하다   thriftily 아끼며

"It is much more difficult to judge oneself than to judge others."

"But you will pardon him on each occasion; for he must be treated thriftily. He is the only one we have."

"I," replied the little prince, "do not like to condemn anyone to death. And now I think I will go on my way."

"그렇다면 너 자신을 재판하도록 하라." 왕이 말했다. "그것이 가장 어려운 일이니까. 남을 판단하는 것보다 자기 자신을 판단하는 것이 훨씬 어려운 일이니라. 자신을 훌륭하게 판단할 수 있다면 그대는 참으로 지혜로운 사람이다." "그럴게요." 어린 왕자가 대답했다. "하지만 판단은 여기가 아니라 다른 데서도 할 수 있는걸요. 꼭 여기 살면서 할 필요는 없어요." "흠! 흠! 집의 별 어딘가에 늙은 쥐 한 마리가 사는 것 같다. 밤마다 녀석의 울음소리가 들리노라. 그대는 그 쥐를 재판하도록 하라. 때때로 사형을 선고해도 좋다. 그러면 그 쥐의 생명이 너에게 달려 있게 될 것이니라. 그러나 매번 사면을 내려야 한다. 그 쥐는 단 한 마리뿐이므로 소중하게 대해야 하느니라." "저는 누구에게도 사형 선고를 내리고 싶지 않아요." 어린 왕자가 대답했다. "이제는 갈 때가 된 것 같아요." "안 된다." 왕이 말했다.

But the little prince, having now completed his preparations for departure, had no wish to grieve the old monarch.

"If Your Majesty wishes to be promptly obeyed," he said, "he should be able to give me a reasonable order. He should be able, for example, to order me to be gone by the end of one minute. It seems to me that conditions are favorable…"

As the king made no answer, the little prince hesitated a moment. Then, with a sigh, he took his leave.

"I make you my Ambassador," the king called out, hastily.

He had a magnificent air of authority.

"The grown-ups are very strange," the little prince said to himself, as he continued on his journey.

어휘   complete 완료하다   preparation 준비   departure 출발   grieve 슬프게 하다
monarch 군주   hesitate 망설이다   sigh 한숨 쉬다   ambassador 대사   hastily
허둥지둥

But the little prince, having now completed his preparations for departure, had no wish to grieve the old monarch.

"I make you my Ambassador," the king called out, hastily.

"The grown-ups are very strange," the little prince said to himself, as he continued on his journey.

어린 왕자는 떠날 준비를 마쳤지만 늙은 왕을 슬프게 하고 싶지 않았다. "폐하의 명령이 즉시 실행되길 원하신다면 사리에 맞는 명을 내려 주세요. 예를 들면 제게 일 분 안에 이 별을 떠나라고 명령하실 수 있겠죠. 제 생각에는 지금 조건이 갖춰진 것 같거든요…" 왕은 아무런 대답도 하지 않았고, 어린 왕자는 잠시 머뭇거리다가 한숨을 쉬고는 별을 떠났다. "그대를 짐의 외교 대사로 임명하노라." 왕이 다급하게 외쳤다. 그는 권력자의 위엄을 내뿜었다. "어른들은 정말 이상해." 어린 왕자가 길을 나서며 중얼거렸다.

The second planet was inhabited by a conceited man.

"Ah! Ah! I am about to receive a visit from an admirer!" he exclaimed from afar, when he first saw the little prince coming.

For, to conceited men, all other men are admirers.

"Good morning," said the little prince. "That is a queer hat you are wearing."

"It is a hat for salutes," the conceited man replied. "It is to raise in salute when people acclaim me. Unfortunately, nobody at all ever passes this way."

어휘 conceited 잘난 척하는 receive 받다 admirer 숭배자 exclaim 외치다
queer 기이한 salute 인사, 경례 acclaim 칭송하다 pass 지나가다

The second planet was inhabited by a conceited man.

"It is a hat for salutes," the conceited man replied.

"Unfortunately, nobody at all ever passes this way."

해석

두 번째 별에는 허영꾼이 살고 있었다. "아! 아! 저기 나를 숭배하는 사람이 찾아오는군!" 어린 왕자를 발견한 그가 저 멀리서 외쳤다. 허영꾼에게는 세상 모든 사람이 자신의 숭배자였다. "안녕하세요." 어린 왕자가 말했다. "특이한 모자를 쓰고 계시네요." "이건 인사용 모자란다." 허영꾼이 대답했다. "사람들이 내게 환호를 보내면 모자를 들어 인사하는 거지. 하지만 안타깝게도 이쪽을 지나가는 사람이 아무도 없어."

"Yes?" said the little prince, who did not understand what the conceited man was talking about.

"Clap your hands, one against the other," the conceited man now directed him.

The little prince clapped his hands. The conceited man raised his hat in a modest salute.

"This is more entertaining than the visit to the king," the little prince said to himself. And he began again to clap his hands, one against the other. The conceited man again raised his hat in salute.

After five minutes of this exercise the little prince grew tired of the game's monotony.

"And what should one do to make the hat come down?" he asked.

But the conceited man did not hear him. Conceited people never hear anything but praise.

어휘 clap one's hands 박수를 치다 directed 지시하다 raise 들어올리다 modest 겸손한
entertaining 재미있는 monotony 단조로움 praise 칭찬, 칭송

The conceited man raised his hat in a modest salute.

After five minutes of this exercise the little prince grew tired of the game's monotony.

Conceited people never hear anything but praise.

"그래요?" 어린 왕자는 그가 하는 말을 이해하지 못했다. "두 손을 마주쳐 손뼉을 쳐 보렴." 허영꾼이 지시를 내렸다. 어린 왕자는 손뼉을 쳤다. 그러자 허영꾼은 모자를 들어 올리며 점잖게 인사했다. "이건 왕을 방문했을 때보다 더 재미있는걸." 어린 왕자가 중얼거렸다. 그는 다시 한쪽 손에 다른 손을 마주치며 손뼉을 쳤다. 허영꾼은 또다시 모자를 들며 인사했다. 오 분쯤 되풀이하자 어린 왕자는 이 단조로운 놀이가 지겨워졌다. "어떻게 하면 그 모자가 떨어지나요?" 어린 왕자가 물었다. 하지만 허영꾼에게는 그 말이 들리지 않았다. 허영심이 많은 사람은 칭찬하는 말밖에 듣지 않는다.

"Do you really admire me very much?" he demanded of the little prince.

"What does that mean--'admire'?"

"To admire means that you regard me as the handsomest, the best-dressed, the richest, and the most intelligent man on this planet."

"But you are the only man on your planet!"

"Do me this kindness. Admire me just the same."

"I admire you," said the little prince, shrugging his shoulders slightly, "but what is there in that to interest you so much?"

And the little prince went away.

"The grown-ups are certainly very odd," he said to himself, as he continued on his journey.

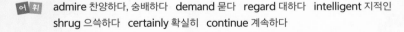

어휘   admire 찬양하다, 숭배하다   demand 묻다   regard 대하다   intelligent 지적인
shrug 으쓱하다   certainly 확실히   continue 계속하다

"To admire means that you regard me as the handsomest, the best-dressed, the richest, and the most intelligent man on this planet."

"But you are the only man on your planet!"

"I admire you," said the little prince, shrugging his shoulders slightly, "but what is there in that to interest you so much?"

"너는 정말로 나를 그렇게 숭배하니?" 그가 어린 왕자에게 물었다. "'숭배'가 뭐예요?" "숭배라는 건 내가 이 별에서 가장 잘 생기고, 가장 옷을 잘 입고, 가장 부유하고, 가장 똑똑한 사람이라고 인정하는 거지." "하지만 이 별에는 아저씨밖에 없잖아요!" "나를 기쁘게 해 주렴. 계속 똑같이 숭배해 줘." "전 아저씨를 숭배해요." 어린 왕자가 어깨를 살짝 으쓱하며 대답했다. "그런데 아저씨는 그걸 왜 그렇게 좋아하는 거예요?" 그리고 어린 왕자는 그 별을 떠났다. "어른들은 정말 너무 이상해." 그가 길을 나서며 중얼거렸다.

The next planet was inhabited by a tippler. This was a very short visit, but it plunged the little prince into deep dejection.

"What are you doing there?" he said to the tippler, whom he found settled down in silence before a collection of empty bottles and also a collection of full bottles.

"I am drinking," replied the tippler, with a lugubrious air. "Why are you drinking?" demanded the little prince.

"So that I may forget," replied the tippler.

 어휘 tippler 술꾼 plunge 떨어져 내리다 dejection 우울함 settle down 자리 잡다
silence 침묵 empty 비어 있는 lugubrious 침울한 forget 잊다

The next planet was inhabited by a tippler.

"Why are you drinking?" demanded the little prince.

"So that I may forget," replied the tippler.

그다음 별에는 주정뱅이가 살고 있었다. 아주 짧은 방문이었지만, 어린 왕자는 깊은 우울함에 빠지고 말았다. "거기서 뭘 하시는 거예요?" 빈 병 한 무더기와 술이 가득 찬 병 한 무더기를 앞에 두고 말없이 앉아 있던 주정뱅이에게 어린 왕자가 물었다. "술을 마시고 있지." 주정뱅이가 침울한 말투로 대꾸했다. "왜 술을 마시는데요?" 어린 왕자가 물었다. "잊으려고." 주정뱅이가 대답했다.

"Forget what?" inquired the little prince, who already was sorry for him.

"Forget that I am ashamed," the tippler confessed, hanging his head.

"Ashamed of what?" insisted the little prince, who wanted to help him.

"Ashamed of drinking!" The tippler brought his speech to an end, and shut himself up in an impregnable silence.

And the little prince went away, puzzled.

"The grown-ups are certainly very, very odd," he said to himself, as he continued on his journey.

어휘 inquire 질문하다 sorry 안타까운 ashamed 부끄러운 confess 고백하다 insist 끈질기게 말하다 impregnable 확고한 puzzled 어리둥절한

"Forget what?" inquired the little prince, who already was sorry for him.

"Forget that I am ashamed," the tippler confessed, hanging his head.

"Ashamed of drinking!" The tippler brought his speech to an end, and shut himself up in an impregnable silence.

"뭘 잊으려는 건데요?" 벌써 측은한 마음이 든 어린 왕자가 물었다. "부끄러움을 잊으려고." 술꾼이 머리를 푹 숙이며 고백하듯 대답했다. "뭐가 부끄러운데요?" 어린 왕자는 그를 돕고 싶었다. "술을 마시는 게 부끄러워!" 주정뱅이는 말을 마치고는 입을 꾹 다문 채 깊은 침묵에 빠졌다. 어린 왕자는 어리둥절한 마음을 안고 그 별을 떠났다. "어른들은 정말 너무, 너무 이상해." 그가 길을 나서며 중얼거렸다.

The fourth planet belonged to a businessman. This man was so much occupied that he did not even raise his head at the little prince's arrival.

"Good morning," the little prince said to him. "Your cigarette has gone out."

"Three and two make five. Five and seven make twelve. Twelve and three make fifteen. Good morning. Fifteen and seven make twenty-two. Twenty-two and six make twenty-eight. I haven't time to light it again. Twenty-six and five make thirty-one. Phew! Then that makes five-hundred-and-one million, six-hundred-twenty-two-thousand, seven-hundred-thirty-one."

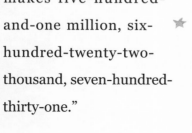

어휘 belong 소유되다 occupied 바쁜 raise one's head 고개를 들다 arrival 도착
cigarette 담배 go out 불이 꺼지다

The fourth planet belonged to a businessman.

This man was so much occupied that he did not even raise his head at the little prince's arrival.

"Good morning," the little prince said to him. "Your cigarette has gone out."

네 번째 별은 사업가의 별이었다. 그는 어찌나 바쁜지 어린 왕자가 찾아왔음에도 고개조차 들지 않았다. "안녕하세요." 어린 왕자가 말했다. "담뱃불이 꺼졌는데요." "셋에 둘을 더하면 다섯, 다섯에 일곱을 더하면 열둘, 열둘에 셋을 더하면 열다섯. 안녕? 열다섯에 일곱을 더하면 스물둘, 스물둘에 여섯을 더하면 스물여덟. 담뱃불을 붙일 시간이 없단다. 스물여섯에 다섯을 더하면 서른하나. 휴! 그럼 5억 162만 2,731이 되는군."

"Five hundred million what?" asked the little prince.

"Eh? Are you still there? Five-hundred-and-one million--I can't stop... I have so much to do! I am concerned with matters of consequence. I don't amuse myself with balderdash. Two and five make seven..."

"Five-hundred-and-one million what?" repeated the little prince, who never in his life had let go of a question once he had asked it.

The businessman raised his head.

"During the fifty-four years that I have inhabited this planet, I have been disturbed only three times. The first time was twenty-two years ago, when some giddy goose fell from goodness knows where. He made the most frightful noise that resounded all over the place, and I made four mistakes in my addition. The second time, eleven years ago, I was disturbed by an attack of rheumatism. I don't get enough exercise. I have no time for loafing. The third time--well, this is it! I was saying, then, five-hundred-and-one millions--"

---

 still 여전히 amuse 즐겁게 하다 balderdash 허튼소리 disturb 방해하다 giddy 경솔한 goose (속어) 바보, 멍청이 frightful 끔찍한 addition 덧셈 loaf 빈둥거리다

"I am concerned with matters of consequence."

_____

_____

"I don't amuse myself with balderdash."

_____

_____

"During the fifty-four years that I have inhabited this planet,
I have been disturbed only three times."

_____

_____

"뭐가 5억이에요?" 어린 왕자가 물었다. "너 아직 거기 있었니? 5억 100만… 내가 일을 멈출 수 없어서… 일이 너무 많거든! 나는 중요한 일을 하는 사람이야. 허튼소리로 시간 낭비를 할 순 없어. 둘에 다섯을 더하면 일곱….." "뭐가 5억 100만 개인가요?" 한 번 질문한 건 절대 포기하지 않는 어린 왕자가 다시 물었다. 사업가가 고개를 들었다. "이 별에 살아온 54년 동안 방해받은 적은 딱 세 번이었어. 첫 번째는 22년 전이었는데, 갑자기 덜떨어진 멍청이가 하늘에서 뚝 떨어졌지. 그놈이 온 별에 울려 퍼지도록 시끄러운 소리를 내는 바람에 덧셈을 네 번이나 틀렸어. 두 번째는 11년 전이었는데, 류머티즘 신경통이 문제였지. 난 평소에 운동을 잘 하지 않거든. 빈둥거릴 시간이 없으니까. 그리고 세 번째는 바로 지금이야! 가만 보자. 내가 방금 5억 100만 하고….."

"Millions of what?"

The businessman suddenly realized that there was no hope of being left in peace until he answered this question.

"Millions of those little objects," he said, "which one sometimes sees in the sky."

"Flies?"

"Oh, no. Little glittering objects."

"Bees?"

"Oh, no. Little golden objects that set lazy men to idle dreaming. As for me, I am concerned with matters of consequence. There is no time for idle dreaming in my life."

"Ah! You mean the stars?"

"Yes, that's it. The stars."

"And what do you do with five-hundred millions of stars?"

어휘 suddenly 갑자기 realize 깨닫다 peace 평화 glittering 반짝이는 bee 벌
lazy 게으른 idle 한가한

The businessman suddenly realized that there was no hope of being left in peace until he answered this question.

"Oh, no. Little golden objects that set lazy men to idle dreaming."

"And what do you do with five-hundred millions of stars?"

"Five-hundred-and-one million, six-hundred-twenty-two thousand, seven-hundred-thirty-one. I am concerned with matters of consequence: I am accurate."

"And what do you do with these stars?"

"What do I do with them?"

"Yes."

"Nothing. I own them."

"You own the stars?"

"Yes."

"But I have already seen a king who--"

"Kings do not *own*, they *reign over*. It is a very different matter."

"And what good does it do you to own the stars?"

"It does me the good of making me rich."

"And what good does it do you to be rich?"

"It makes it possible for me to buy more stars, if any are discovered."

어휘 accurate 정확한 own 소유하다 reign 통치하다 rich 부유한 possible 가능한
buy 사다 discover 발견하다

"And what do you do with these stars?"

"It does me the good of making me rich."

"It makes it possible for me to buy more stars, if any are discovered."

"This man," the little prince said to himself, "reasons a little like my poor tippler…"

Nevertheless, he still had some more questions.

"How is it possible for one to own the stars?"

"To whom do they belong?" the businessman retorted, peevishly.

"I don't know. To nobody."

"Then they belong to me, because I was the first person to think of it."

"Is that all that is necessary?"

"Certainly. When you find a diamond that belongs to nobody, it is yours. When you discover an island that belongs to nobody, it is yours. When you get an idea before any one else, you take out a patent on it: it is yours. So with me: I own the stars, because nobody else before me ever thought of owning them."

"Yes, that is true," said the little prince. "And what do you do with them?"

---

 reason 생각하다 possible 가능한 retort 쏘아붙이다 peevishly 언짢게
necessary 필요한 take out 취득하다 patent 특허

"This man," the little prince said to himself, "reasons a little like my poor tippler..."

"Certainly. When you find a diamond that belongs to nobody, it is yours."

"So with me: I own the stars, because nobody else before me ever thought of owning them."

"이 사람은" 어린 왕자가 중얼거렸다. "불쌍한 주정뱅이 아저씨랑 조금 비슷한 것 같아…." 어쨌든 그는 질문을 계속했다. "별들을 어떻게 소유한다는 거예요?" "저 별들은 누구 거지?" 사업가가 언짢은 기색으로 툴툴거렸다. "몰라요. 누구의 것도 아니겠죠." "그러니까 내 거야. 별을 갖는다는 생각을 맨 처음 한 사람이 바로 나니까." "그렇다고 해서 아저씨 것이 되나요?" "그럼. 네가 임자 없는 다이아몬드를 발견한다면 그건 네 거야. 임자 없는 섬을 발견해도 마찬가지지. 네가 어떤 좋은 생각을 최초로 떠올린다면 특허권을 갖게 돼. 나도 똑같단다. 나보다 먼저 별들을 소유하겠다고 생각한 사람이 없었기 때문에 내가 소유하는 거야." "그건 그렇네요." 어린 왕자가 말했다. "그럼 아저씨는 그 별들을 가지고 뭘 하실 거예요?"

"I administer them," replied the businessman. "I count them and recount them. It is difficult. But I am a man who is naturally interested in matters of consequence."

The little prince was still not satisfied.

"If I owned a silk scarf," he said, "I could put it around my neck and take it away with me. If I owned a flower, I could pluck that flower and take it away with me. But you cannot pluck the stars from heaven..."

"No. But I can put them in the bank."

"Whatever does that mean?"

"That means that I write the number of my stars on a little paper. And then I put this paper in a drawer and lock it with a key."

"And that is all?"

"That is enough," said the businessman.

---

 administer 관리하다 count 숫자를 세다 naturally 본질적으로 put around 두르다
pluck 뽑다 drawer 서랍 lock 잠그다

"If I owned a flower, I could pluck that flower and take it away with me."

"But you cannot pluck the stars from heaven..."

"That means that I write the number of my stars on a little paper."

"그것들을 관리하지." 사업가가 대답했다. "숫자를 세고 또 세는 거야. 힘든 일이지만 나는 중요한 일에 워낙 관심이 많거든." 하지만 어린 왕자는 여전히 궁금했다. "만약 내게 실크 스카프가 있다면 그걸 목에 두르고 다닐 수 있어요. 꽃을 소유한다면 꺾어서 가지고 다닐 수 있겠죠. 하지만 아저씨는 하늘에서 별을 딸 수 없잖아요…" "맞아. 하지만 그것들을 은행에 맡길 수는 있지." "그게 대체 무슨 말이에요?" "내 별의 숫자들을 작은 종이에 적는 거야. 그리고 종이를 서랍에 넣고 열쇠로 잠그는 거지." "그게 다예요?" "그게 다야." 사업가가 말했다.

"It is entertaining," thought the little prince. "It is rather poetic. But it is of no great consequence."

On matters of consequence, the little prince had ideas which were very different from those of the grown-ups.

"I myself own a flower," he continued his conversation with the businessman, "which I water every day. I own three volcanoes, which I clean out every week (for I also clean out the one that is extinct; one never knows). It is of some use to my volcanoes, and it is of some use to my flower, that I own them. But you are of no use to the stars..."

The businessman opened his mouth, but he found nothing to say in answer. And the little prince went away.

"The grown-ups are certainly altogether extraordinary," he said simply, talking to himself as he continued on his journey.

어휘 entertaining 흥미로운 poetic 시적인 continue 이어가다 conversation 대화
extinct 활동을 멈춘 of use 쓸모 있는 of no use 쓸모 없는

"It is rather poetic. But it is of no great consequence."

"But you are of no use to the stars..."

The businessman opened his mouth, but he found nothing to say in answer.

'흥미로운걸.' 어린 왕자는 생각했다. '시적인 느낌이야. 하지만 그렇게 중요한 일 같진 않아.' 중요한 일에 대해서, 어린 왕자는 어른들과 아주 다른 생각을 갖고 있었다. "저는 꽃 한 송이를 갖고 있어요." 그가 사업가를 향해 말을 이었다. "매일 그 꽃에 물을 주죠. 세 개의 화산도 갖고 있는데, 매주 청소를 해요(불 꺼진 사화산까지 청소해요. 어떻게 될지는 아무도 모르는 일이니까요.) 그건 내가 소유한 화산과 꽃에게 도움이 되는 일이에요. 하지만 아저씨는 아저씨의 별에게 아무런 도움이 되지 않아요…." 사업가는 무슨 말을 하려고 했으나 할 말을 찾지 못했다. 어린 왕자는 그 별을 떠났다. "어른들은 하나같이 너무 이상해." 그가 길을 나서며 담담하게 중얼거렸다.

The fifth planet was very strange. It was the smallest of all. There was just enough room on it for a street lamp and a lamplighter. The little prince was not able to reach any explanation of the use of a street lamp and a lamplighter, somewhere in the heavens, on a planet which had no people, and not one house. But he said to himself, nevertheless:

"It may well be that this man is absurd. But he is not so absurd as the king, the conceited man, the businessman, and the tippler. For at least his work has some meaning. When he lights his street lamp, it is as if he brought one more star to life, or one flower. When he puts out his lamp, he sends the flower, or the star, to sleep. That is a beautiful occupation. And since it is beautiful, it is truly useful."

strange 이상한 room 공간 reach ~에 이르다 explanation 설명 lamplighter 가로등지기 absurd 터무니없는 meaning 의미 occupation 직업

The little prince was not able to reach any explanation of the use of a street lamp and a lamplighter, somewhere in the heavens, on a planet which had no people, and not one house.

"When he puts out his lamp, he sends the flower, or the star, to sleep." That is a beautiful occupation.

다섯 번째 별은 무척 이상한 별이었다. 그것은 지금까지 본 별 가운데 가장 작았는데, 가로등 하나와 가로등지기 한 명이 서 있을 자리밖에 없었다. 우주 한구석에 있는, 집도 사람도 없는 별에 가로등과 가로등지기가 왜 필요한지 어린 왕자는 도무지 이해할 수 없었다. 어쨌든 그는 이렇게 중얼거렸다. "이 사람은 어리석을지도 몰라. 하지만 왕이나 허영꾼, 사업가, 주정뱅이보다는 덜 어리석지. 적어도 그가 하는 일에는 의미가 있으니까. 그가 가로등을 켜는 건 별 하나, 꽃 한 송이가 더 태어나는 것과 같아. 그가 가로등을 끄면 꽃이나 별이 잠에 들지. 그건 멋진 일이야. 멋진 만큼 유용한 일이기도 하고."

When he arrived on the planet he respectfully saluted the lamplighter.

"Good morning. Why have you just put out your lamp?"

"Those are the orders," replied the lamplighter. "Good morning."

"What are the orders?"

"The orders are that I put out my lamp. Good evening."

And he lighted his lamp again.

"But why have you just lighted it again?"

"Those are the orders," replied the lamplighter.

"I do not understand," said the little prince.

"There is nothing to understand," said the lamplighter. "Orders are orders. Good morning."

And he put out his lamp.

Then he mopped his forehead with a handkerchief decorated with red squares.

어휘   arrive 도착하다   respectfully 공손히   salute 인사하다   reply 대답하다   order 명령 put out 불을 끄다   mop 닦다   forehead 이마

"Good morning. Why have you just put out your lamp?"

_____

_____

"Those are the orders," replied the lamplighter. "Good morning."

_____

_____

"The orders are that I put out my lamp. Good evening."

_____

_____

별에 도착한 어린 왕자는 가로등지기에게 공손하게 인사했다. "안녕하세요? 어째서 방금 가로등을 끄신 건가요?" "명령이니까." 가로등지기가 대답했다. "안녕." "무슨 명령인데요?" "이 가로등을 끄는 거지. 좋은 저녁이구나." 그리고 그는 다시 가로등을 켰다. "그럼 왜 다시 가로등을 켜신 거예요?" "그게 바로 명령이거든" 가로등지기가 대답했다. "이해가 되지 않아요." 어린 왕자가 말했다. "이해하고 말 게 없어." 가로등지기가 말했다. "명령은 명령이야. 좋은 아침이구나." 그리고 그는 다시 가로등을 껐다. 그러더니 그는 붉은 격자무늬 손수건으로 이마에 맺힌 땀을 닦았다.

"I follow a terrible profession. In the old days it was reasonable. I put the lamp out in the morning, and in the evening I lighted it again. I had the rest of the day for relaxation and the rest of the night for sleep."

"And the orders have been changed since that time?"

"The orders have not been changed," said the lamplighter. "That is the tragedy! From year to year the planet has turned more rapidly and the orders have not been changed!"

"Then what?" asked the little prince.

"Then--the planet now makes a complete turn every minute, and I no longer have a single second for repose. Once every minute I have to light my lamp and put it out!"

"That is very funny! A day lasts only one minute, here where you live!"

"It is not funny at all!" said the lamplighter. "While we have been talking together a month has gone by."

"A month?"

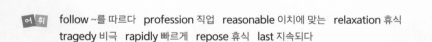

어휘 　follow ~를 따르다 profession 직업 reasonable 이치에 맞는 relaxation 휴식
tragedy 비극 rapidly 빠르게 repose 휴식 last 지속되다

"I put the lamp out in the morning, and in the evening I lighted it again."

"From year to year the planet has turned more rapidly and the orders have not been changed!"

"While we have been talking together a month has gone by."

"나는 끔찍한 직업을 갖고 있어. 예전에는 그래도 할 만했지. 아침이면 가로등을 끄고 저녁이면 가로등을 켰거든. 나머지 낮에는 쉬고 밤에는 잠을 잤어." "그럼 그 후에 명령이 바뀌었나요?" "명령은 바뀌지 않았어." 가로등지기가 말했다. "그게 바로 비극이야! 이 별은 매년 점점 빨리 도는데 명령이 바뀌지 않으니 말이야!" "그럼 어떻게 되는 거예요?" 어린 왕자가 물었다. "지금 이 별은 일 분에 한 번씩 도니까 잠시도 쉴 시간이 없어. 일 분에 한 번씩 가로등을 켰다 껐다 해야 하지!" "정말 웃기네요! 아저씨네 별에서는 하루가 일 분이라는 거잖아요!" "전혀 웃기지 않아." 가로등지기가 말했다. "우리가 이야기를 나누는 사이에 벌써 한 달이 흘렀단다." "한 달이라고요?"

"Yes, a month. Thirty minutes. Thirty days. Good evening."

And he lighted his lamp again.

As the little prince watched him, he felt that he loved this lamplighter who was so faithful to his orders. He remembered the sunsets which he himself had gone to seek, in other days, merely by pulling up his chair; and he wanted to help his friend.

"You know," he said, "I can tell you a way you can rest whenever you want to..."

"I always want to rest," said the lamplighter.

For it is possible for a man to be faithful and lazy at the same time. The little prince went on with his explanation:

"Your planet is so small that three strides will take you all the way around it. To be always in the sunshine, you need only walk along rather slowly. When you want to rest, you will walk--and the day will last as long as you like."

"That doesn't do me much good," said the lamplighter. "The one thing I love in life is to sleep."

어휘 watch 지켜보다 faithful 충성스러운 merely 단지 lazy 게으른 stride 성큼성큼 걷다
sunshine 햇빛

As the little prince watched him, he felt that he loved this lamplighter who was so faithful to his orders.

"When you want to rest, you will walk—and the day will last as long as you like."

"The one thing I love in life is to sleep."

 해석

"그래. 한 달. 30분이니까 30일이지. 좋은 저녁이구나." 그리고 그는 다시 가로등을 켰다. 어린 왕자는 가로등지기를 바라보았다. 그는 주어진 일을 이토록 성실히 하는 가로등지기가 좋았다. 문득 의자를 옮기며 석양을 계속 바라보던 시절이 생각났다. 어린 왕자는 친구를 도와주고 싶었다. "있잖아요." 그가 말했다. "쉬고 싶을 때마다 쉴 수 있는 방법을 알려드릴게요…" "난 언제나 쉬고 싶어." 가로등지기가 대답했다. 사람은 누구나 성실한 동시에 게으른 면을 지닌 법이다. 어린 왕자는 그에게 설명했다. "아저씨 별은 너무 작아서 세 발자국만 걸어도 한 바퀴를 돌 수 있어요. 천천히 걷기만 해도 하루 종일 햇빛 속에 있을 수 있는 거죠. 쉬고 싶으실 땐 걸어 보세요. 그러면 낮의 길이를 원하는 만큼 늘일 수 있을 거예요." "그건 별로 도움이 안 되는걸." 가로등지기가 말했다. "내가 무엇보다 원하는 건 잠을 자는 거거든."

"Then you're unlucky," said the little prince.

"I am unlucky," said the lamplighter. "Good morning."

And he put out his lamp.

"That man," said the little prince to himself, as he continued farther on his journey, "that man would be scorned by all the others: by the king, by the conceited man, by the tippler, by the businessman. Nevertheless he is the only one of them all who does not seem to me ridiculous. Perhaps that is because he is thinking of something else besides himself."

He breathed a sigh of regret, and said to himself, again:

"That man is the only one of them all whom I could have made my friend. But his planet is indeed too small. There is no room on it for two people…"

What the little prince did not dare confess was that he was sorry most of all to leave this planet, because it was blest every day with 1440 sunsets!

어휘 unlucky 불행한 put out 불을 끄다 scorn 경멸하다 nevertheless 그럼에도 불구하고
ridiculous 어리석은 sigh 한숨 쉬다 dare 감히 confess 고백하다 bless 축복

"Nevertheless he is the only one of them all who does not seem to me ridiculous."

What the little prince did not dare confess was that he was sorry most of all to leave this planet, because it was blest every day with 1440 sunsets!

The sixth planet was ten times larger than the last one. It was inhabited by an old gentleman who wrote voluminous books.

"Oh, look! Here is an explorer!" he exclaimed to himself when he saw the little prince coming.

The little prince sat down on the table and panted a little. He had already traveled so much and so far!

"Where do you come from?" the old gentleman said to him.

"What is that big book?" said the little prince. "What are you doing?"

어휘 last 직전의 gentleman 신사 voluminous 방대한 explorer 탐험가 pant 헐떡이다
already 이미 travel 여행하다

It was inhabited by an old gentleman who wrote voluminous books.

"Oh, look! Here is an explorer!" he exclaimed to himself when he saw the little prince coming.

The little prince sat down on the table and panted a little.

"I am a geographer," said the old gentleman.

"What is a geographer?" asked the little prince.

"A geographer is a scholar who knows the location of all the seas, rivers, towns, mountains, and deserts."

"That is very interesting," said the little prince. "Here at last is a man who has a real profession!" And he cast a look around him at the planet of the geographer. It was the most magnificent and stately planet that he had ever seen.

"Your planet is very beautiful," he said. "Has it any oceans?"

"I couldn't tell you," said the geographer.

"Ah!" The little prince was disappointed. "Has it any mountains?"

"I couldn't tell you," said the geographer.

"And towns, and rivers, and deserts?"

"I couldn't tell you that, either."

"But you are a geographer!"

어휘 geographer 지리학자 scholar 학자 location 장소 river 강 desert 사막 stately 위풍당당한 ocean 바다, 대양 disappoint 실망시키다

"A geographer is a scholar who knows the location of all the seas, rivers, towns, mountains, and deserts."

And he cast a look around him at the planet of the geographer.

It was the most magnificent and stately planet that he had ever seen.

 해 석

"난 지리학자란다." 노신사가 대답했다. "지리학자가 뭔데요?" 어린 왕자가 물었다. "지리학자란 모든 바다와 강, 마을, 산, 사막의 위치를 알고 있는 학자이지." "그거 정말 흥미롭네요." 어린 왕자가 말했다. '마침내 직업다운 직업을 가진 사람을 만났군!' 그는 지리학자의 별을 한 바퀴 둘러보았다. 그처럼 장엄하고 위풍당당한 별은 본 적이 없었다. "이 별은 정말 멋져요." 그가 말했다. "이곳에 바다도 있나요?" "그건 알 수 없단다." 지리학자가 말했다. "오!" 어린 왕자는 실망했다. "그럼 산은 있나요?" "그것도 알 수 없단다." 지리학자가 말했다. "그럼 마을이나 강, 사막은요?" "역시 알 수 없단다." "하지만 아저씨는 지리학자잖아요!"

"Exactly," the geographer said. "But I am not an explorer. I haven't a single explorer on my planet. It is not the geographer who goes out to count the towns, the rivers, the mountains, the seas, the oceans, and the deserts. The geographer is much too important to go loafing about. He does not leave his desk. But he receives the explorers in his study. He asks them questions, and he notes down what they recall of their travels. And if the recollections of any one among them seem interesting to him, the geographer orders an inquiry into that explorer's moral character."

"Why is that?"

"Because an explorer who told lies would bring disaster on the books of the geographer. So would an explorer who drank too much."

"Why is that?" asked the little prince.

"Because intoxicated men see double. Then the geographer would note down two mountains in a place where there was only one."

어휘 count 숫자를 세다 loaf about 빈둥거리다 leave 떠나다 receive 받다 recall 떠올리다 inquiry 질문하다 moral character 도덕성 disaster 재난 intoxicated (술, 마약에) 취한

"It is not the geographer who goes out to count the towns, the rivers, the mountains, the seas, the oceans, and the deserts."

"The geographer is much too important to go loafing about."

"Because an explorer who told lies would bring disaster on the books of the geographer."

"그렇지." 지리학자가 말했다. "하지만 난 탐험가가 아니란다. 내 별에는 탐험가가 한 명도 없어. 마을과 강, 산, 바다, 대양을 세러 다니는 건 지리학자의 일이 아니야. 지리학자는 한가하게 돌아다니기에 너무 중요한 사람이거든. 우리는 결코 책상을 떠날 수 없지. 그 대신 탐험가가 가져온 자료를 받고, 그들에게 질문을 던지고, 그들이 여행하며 쌓은 기억을 기록하는 거야. 탐험가의 기억 중에 흥미로운 것이 있다면 지리학자는 그의 행실을 조사한단다." "왜요?" "탐험가가 거짓말을 하면 지리학자가 쓴 책에 큰 문제가 생기거든. 탐험가가 술을 너무 많이 마셔도 그렇고." "그건 왜죠?" 어린 왕자가 물었다. "술에 취한 사람에게는 뭐든지 둘로 보이거든. 그러면 지리학자는 산이 하나밖에 없는 곳에다 산이 두 개 있다고 기록하게 되지."

"I know some one," said the little prince, "who would make a bad explorer."

"That is possible. Then, when the moral character of the explorer is shown to be good, an inquiry is ordered into his discovery."

"One goes to see it?"

"No. That would be too complicated. But one requires the explorer to furnish proofs. For example, if the discovery in question is that of a large mountain, one requires that large stones be brought back from it."

The geographer was suddenly stirred to excitement.

"But you--you come from far away! You are an explorer! You shall describe your planet to me!"

And, having opened his big register, the geographer sharpened his pencil. The recitals of explorers are put down first in pencil. One waits until the explorer has furnished proofs, before putting them down in ink.

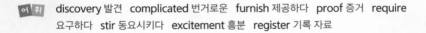

어휘 discovery 발견 complicated 번거로운 furnish 제공하다 proof 증거 require 요구하다 stir 동요시키다 excitement 흥분 register 기록 자료

"Then, when the moral character of the explorer is shown to be good, an inquiry is ordered into his discovery."

"For example, if the discovery in question is that of a large mountain, one requires that large stones be brought back from it."

"You shall describe your planet to me!"

"저도 그런 사람을 알고 있어요." 어린 왕자가 말했다. "그 사람은 무능한 탐험가가 되겠네요." "그럴 수 있지. 그러니 탐험가의 행실이 바르다고 판단했을 때만 그의 발견을 조사하는 거야." "지리학자가 직접 가서 보나요?" "아니. 그건 너무 번거롭거든. 대신 탐험가에게 증거를 제시하라고 요구하지. 예를 들어, 커다란 산을 발견한 것에 대한 증거물로는 그곳에서 채취한 커다란 돌멩이를 요구한단다." 그러더니 그는 갑자기 흥분했다. "그런데 너도 멀리서 왔잖니! 너도 탐험가야! 네가 살던 별은 어떤 곳인지 내게 설명해다오!" 지리학자는 커다란 노트를 펴고는 연필을 깎았다. 처음에는 탐험가의 이야기를 연필로 적고, 그가 증거를 가져오길 기다렸다가 잉크로 다시 적기 위해서였다.

"Well?" said the geographer expectantly.

"Oh, where I live," said the little prince, "it is not very interesting. It is all so small. I have three volcanoes. Two volcanoes are active and the other is extinct. But one never knows."

"One never knows," said the geographer.

"I have also a flower."

"We do not record flowers," said the geographer.

"Why is that? The flower is the most beautiful thing on my planet!"

"We do not record them," said the geographer, "because they are ephemeral."

"What does that mean--'ephemeral'?"

---

 expectantly 기대감에 찬 interesting 흥미로운 active 활동중인 extinct 활동하지 않는 record 기록하다 ephemeral 덧없는, 단명하는

"We do not record flowers," said the geographer.

"Why is that? The flower is the most beautiful thing on my planet!"

"We do not record them," said the geographer, "because they are ephemeral."

"시작해볼까?" 지리학자가 기대에 가득한 목소리로 말했다. "음, 제 별은 별로 흥미로울 게 없어요." 어린 왕자가 말했다. "너무 작거든요. 화산이 셋 있는데, 두 개는 활화산이고 하나는 사화산이에요. 하지만 어떻게 될지는 아무도 모르는 일이죠." "그래. 아무도 모르는 일이지." 지리학자가 말했다. "우리 별에는 꽃도 한 송이 있어요." "꽃은 기록하지 않는단다." "어째서죠? 그 꽃은 별 전체에서 가장 아름다운 존재인데!" "그런 건 기록하지 않아." 지리학자가 말했다. "덧없는 존재니까." "'덧없는 존재'가 뭐예요?"

"Geographies," said the geographer, "are the books which, of all books, are most concerned with matters of consequence. They never become old-fashioned. It is very rarely that a mountain changes its position. It is very rarely that an ocean empties itself of its waters. We write of eternal things."

"But extinct volcanoes may come to life again," the little prince interrupted. "What does that mean--'ephemeral'?"

"Whether volcanoes are extinct or alive, it comes to the same thing for us," said the geographer. "The thing that matters to us is the mountain. It does not change."

"But what does that mean--'ephemeral'?" repeated the little prince, who never in his life had let go of a question, once he had asked it.

"It means, 'which is in danger of speedy disappearance.'"

"Is my flower in danger of speedy disappearance?"

"Certainly it is."

---

 geography 지리학 old-fashioned 구식의 rarely 거의 ~하지 않는 eternal 영원한
interrupt 끼어들다 repeat 반복하다 speedy 빠른 disappearance 사라짐

"But what does that mean--'ephemeral'?" repeated the little prince, who never in his life had let go of a question, once he had asked it.

"It means, 'which is in danger of speedy disappearance.'"

"Is my flower in danger of speedy disappearance?"

"지리책은 모든 책 중에 가장 중요하다고 여겨지는 책이야." 지리학자가 말했다. "결코 시대에 뒤떨어지지 않지. 산의 위치가 바뀌는 일은 거의 없거든. 바다가 말라 버리는 일도 마찬가지고. 우리는 영원한 것들을 기록한단다." "하지만 사화산도 언젠가 활동을 시작할 수 있어요." 어린 왕자가 끼어들었다. "그리고 '덧없는 존재'가 뭐예요?" "사화산이든 활화산이든 우리에겐 모두 똑같아." 지리학자가 말했다. "중요한 건 화산 그 자체지. 그건 변하지 않으니까." "그러면 '덧없는 존재'는 뭐예요?" 한 번 던진 질문은 절대 포기하지 않는 어린 왕자가 다시 물었다. "그건 '언제라도 사라질 위험에 처한 것'이라는 뜻이란다." "제 꽃이 언제라도 사라질 위험에 처해 있나요?" "당연히 그렇지."

"My flower is ephemeral," the little prince said to himself, "and she has only four thorns to defend herself against the world. And I have left her on my planet, all alone!"

That was his first moment of regret. But he took courage once more.

"What place would you advise me to visit now?" he asked.

"The planet Earth," replied the geographer. "It has a good reputation." And the little prince went away, thinking of his flower.

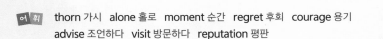

어휘   thorn 가시 alone 홀로 moment 순간 regret 후회 courage 용기
advise 조언하다 visit 방문하다 reputation 평판

"My flower is ephemeral," the little prince said to himself.

"And I have left her on my planet, all alone!"

"The planet Earth," replied the geographer. "It has a good reputation."

"내 꽃은 덧없는 존재야." 어린 왕자가 중얼거렸다. "세상으로부터 자신을 지킬 무기라곤 네 개의 가시밖에 없어. 그런데 나는 그 꽃을 별에 홀로 버려두고 왔구나!" 그 순간 어린 왕자는 처음으로 후회하는 마음이 들었다. 그러나 그는 다시 용기를 냈다. "내가 가볼 만한 곳을 추천해 주시겠어요?" "지구라는 행성을 추천하마." 지리학자가 대답했다. "평판이 좋은 곳이거든." 자신의 꽃을 생각하며, 어린 왕자는 그 별을 떠났다.

So then the seventh planet was the Earth. The Earth is not just an ordinary planet! One can count, there, 111 kings (not forgetting, to be sure, the Negro kings among them), 7000 geographers, 900,000 businessmen, 7,500,000 tipplers, 311,000,000 conceited men--that is to say, about 2,000,000,000 grown-ups.

To give you an idea of the size of the Earth, I will tell you that before the invention of electricity it was necessary to maintain, over the whole of the six continents, a veritable army of 462,511 lamplighters for the street lamps.

The Earth is not just an ordinary planet!

To give you an idea of the size of the Earth, I will tell you that before the invention of electricity it was necessary to maintain, over the whole of the six continents, a veritable army of 462,511 lamplighters for the street lamps.

그리하여 일곱 번째 별은 지구가 되었다. 지구는 그냥 평범한 별이 아니었다! 그곳에는 111명의 왕(물론 흑인 왕도 포함한 수치다), 7,000명의 지리학자, 90만 명의 사업가, 750만 명의 주정뱅이가 살았으며, 허영꾼은 3억 1,100만 명이나 살고 있었다. 다시 말해서, 약 20억 명의 어른들이 사는 곳이었다. 전기가 발명되기 전까지 여섯 대륙을 통틀어 46만 2,511명이나 되는 가로등지기 군단을 유지해야 했다는 사실을 들으면 지구가 얼마나 큰 별인지 감이 올 것이다.

Seen from a slight distance, that would make a splendid spectacle. The movements of this army would be regulated like those of the ballet in the opera. First would come the turn of the lamplighters of New Zealand and Australia. Having set their lamps alight, these would go off to sleep. Next, the lamplighters of China and Siberia would enter for their steps in the dance, and then they too would be waved back into the wings. After that would come the turn of the lamplighters of Russia and the Indies; then those of Africa and Europe; then those of South America; then those of North America. And never would they make a mistake in the order of their entry upon the stage. It would be magnificent.

Only the man who was in charge of the single lamp at the North Pole, and his colleague who was responsible for the single lamp at the South Pole--only these two would live free from toil and care: they would be busy twice a year.

어휘 distance 거리 splendid 눈부신 spectacle 장관 regulate 통제하다 wing (무대 양쪽) 끝
order 순서 entry 등장 colleague 동료 be responsible for ~에 책임이 있는 toil 피
땀 흘려 일하다

Seen from a slight distance, that would make a splendid spectacle.

The movements of this army would be regulated like those of the ballet in the opera.

And never would they make a mistake in the order of their entry upon the stage.

조금 멀리 떨어져서 보면 그것은 눈부신 장관을 연출했다. 가로등지기 군단의 움직임은 오페라 극장의 발레단처럼 질서정연했다. 처음은 뉴질랜드와 오스트레일리아의 가로등지기였다. 그들은 가로등을 켠 뒤 잠을 자러 갔다. 그다음 중국과 시베리아의 가로등지기들이 군무에 합류했다가 역시 무대 뒤로 퇴장했다. 그러면 러시아와 인도의 차례가 왔고 아프리카와 유럽이 뒤를 이었다. 그다음은 남아메리카와 북아메리카 차례였다. 그들 중 누구도 무대에 등장하는 순서를 틀리지 않았다. 그것은 장엄한 광경이었다. 고된 노동에서 자유로운 것은 단 하나뿐인 가로등을 책임지는 북극의 가로등지기와 역시 하나뿐인 가로등을 담당하는 그의 동료, 남극의 가로등지기뿐이었다. 두 사람은 1년에 딱 두 차례만 바쁘게 일했다.

When one wishes to play the wit, he sometimes wanders a little from the truth. I have not been altogether honest in what I have told you about the lamplighters. And I realize that I run the risk of giving a false idea of our planet to those who do not know it. Men occupy a very small place upon the Earth. If the two billion inhabitants who people its surface were all to stand upright and somewhat crowded together, as they do for some big public assembly, they could easily be put into one public square twenty miles long and twenty miles wide. All humanity could be piled up on a small Pacific islet.

여휘   wit 재치   wander (길에서) 벗어나다   altogether 전부   risk 위험   false 잘못된 occupy 차지하다   surface 표면   public assembly 군중 집회   square 광장 islet 작은 섬

When one wishes to play the wit, he sometimes wanders a little from the truth.

I have not been altogether honest in what I have told you about the lamplighters.

Men occupy a very small place upon the Earth.

위트 있는 이야기를 하다 보면 때로 진실에서 조금 멀어지곤 한다. 가로등 켜는 사람들에 대한 내 이야기가 완전한 진실이라고 하기는 어렵다. 지구를 잘 모르는 사람 입장에서 보면 잘못된 생각을 갖게 만들 수 있는 이야기였다. 지구에서 인간이 차지하고 있는 면적은 매우 작다. 만약 지구에 사는 20억 명이 대규모 집회라도 열기 위해 한 장소에 모인다면 가로세로로 30km쯤 되는 공간에 전부 들어갈 것이다. 그들 모두를 태평양의 작은 섬에 쌓아둘 수도 있다.

The grown-ups, to be sure, will not believe you when you tell them that. They imagine that they fill a great deal of space. They fancy themselves as important as the baobabs. You should advise them, then, to make their own calculations. They adore figures, and that will please them. But do not waste your time on this extra task. It is unnecessary. You have, I know, confidence in me.

When the little prince arrived on the Earth, he was very much surprised not to see any people. He was beginning to be afraid he had come to the wrong planet, when a coil of gold, the color of the moonlight, flashed across the sand.

어휘 believe 믿다 imagine 생각하다 fill 채우다 fancy (사실과 다르게) 믿다 calculation 계산 confidence 신뢰 coil 고리, 또아리 sand 모래

The grown-ups, to be sure, will not believe you when you tell them that.

They imagine that they fill a great deal of space.

When the little prince arrived on the Earth, he was very much surprised not to see any people.

물론 어른들에게 이런 말을 해도 믿지 않을 것이다. 그들은 스스로 매우 많은 자리를 차지한다고 생각한다. 자기 자신이 바오바브나무처럼 중요하다고 착각하는 것이다. 그럴 때는 그들에게 계산해 보라고 조언할 수 있다. 숫자를 좋아하는 어른들은 기뻐할 것이다. 하지만 여러분은 이런 자질구레한 일에 시간을 낭비하지 말라. 쓸데없는 짓이니까. 나는 여러분이 이미 나를 믿는다는 사실을 알고 있다. 지구에 막 도착한 어린 왕자는 사람이 하나도 보이지 않아 놀랐다. 실수로 다른 별을 찾아온 게 아닐까 걱정이 들기 시작했을 때, 모랫바닥 속에서 달빛을 닮은 금색 또아리가 나타났다.

"Good evening," said the little prince courteously.

"Good evening," said the snake.

"What planet is this on which I have come down?" asked the little prince.

"This is the Earth; this is Africa," the snake answered.

"Ah! Then there are no people on the Earth?"

"This is the desert. There are no people in the desert. The Earth is large," said the snake.

The little prince sat down on a stone, and raised his eyes toward the sky.

"I wonder," he said, "whether the stars are set alight in heaven so that one day each one of us may find his own again... Look at my planet. It is right there above us. But how far away it is!"

"It is beautiful," the snake said. "What has brought you here?"

"I have been having some trouble with a flower," said the little prince.

어휘   courteously 예의 바르게 come down 내려오다 answer 대답하다 toward ~를 향해
set alight 불을 붙이다 find 찾다 above ~의 위에

"This is the desert. There are no people in the desert. The Earth is large,"

"I wonder," he said, "whether the stars are set alight in heaven so that one day each one of us may find his own again..."

"I have been having some trouble with a flower."

"안녕." 어린 왕자는 정중하게 말을 걸었다. "안녕." 뱀이 대답했다. "내가 도착한 이 별이 무슨 별이니?" 어린 왕자가 물었다. "여긴 지구야. 이곳은 아프리카고." "아, 그러면 지구에는 사람이 없니?" "여기가 사막이라 그래. 사막에는 사람이 살지 않아. 지구는 넓거든." 뱀이 대답했다. 어린 왕자는 바위에 앉은 채 눈을 들어 하늘을 바라보았다. "별이 하늘에서 빛을 밝히는 건." 그가 말했다. "언젠가 우리가 각자의 별을 다시 찾을지도 몰라서일까? 내가 살던 별을 봐. 바로 우리 위에 있어. 하지만 정말 멀리 떨어져 있지!" "아름답구나." 뱀이 말했다. "그런데 여긴 뭐 하러 왔니?" "어떤 꽃하고 문제가 좀 있었어." 어린 왕자가 대답했다.

"Ah!" said the snake.

And they were both silent.

"Where are the men?" the little prince at last took up the conversation again.

"It is a little lonely in the desert..."

"It is also lonely among men," the snake said.

The little prince gazed at him for a long time.

"You are a funny animal," he said at last. "You are no thicker than a finger..."

"But I am more powerful than the finger of a king," said the snake.

The little prince smiled.

"You are not very powerful. You haven't even any feet. You cannot even travel..."

"I can carry you farther than any ship could take you," said the snake.

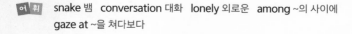

어휘 snake 뱀 conversation 대화 lonely 외로운 among ~의 사이에
gaze at ~을 쳐다보다

"It is a little lonely in the desert..."

"It is also lonely among men," the snake said.

"I can carry you farther than any ship could take you," said the snake.

"그렇군!" 뱀이 말했다. 그리고 둘은 침묵했다. "사람들은 어디에 있어?" 어린 왕자가 마침내 대화를 이어갔다. "사막은 조금 외롭구나…." "사람들 사이에 있어도 외로운 건 마찬가지야." 뱀이 말했다. 어린 왕자는 그를 한참 동안 바라보았다. "넌 재미있는 동물이네." 입을 연 그가 말했다. "손가락처럼 가늘고…." "그래도 난 왕의 손가락보다 더 힘이 세지." 뱀이 말했다. 어린 왕자는 미소 지었다. "넌 힘이 세지 않아. 발도 없잖아. 여행을 하려 해도…." "난 너를 세상 어떤 배보다도 멀리 보내 줄 수 있어." 뱀이 말했다.

He twined himself around the little prince's ankle, like a golden bracelet.

"Whomever I touch, I send back to the earth from whence he came," the snake spoke again. "But you are innocent and true, and you come from a star..."

The little prince made no reply.

"You move me to pity--you are so weak on this Earth made of granite," the snake said. "I can help you, some day, if you grow too homesick for your own planet. I can--"

"Oh! I understand you very well," said the little prince. "But why do you always speak in riddles?"

"I solve them all," said the snake.

And they were both silent.

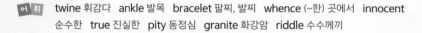

어휘   twine 휘감다   ankle 발목   bracelet 팔찌, 발찌   whence (~한) 곳에서   innocent 순수한   true 진실한   pity 동정심   granite 화강암   riddle 수수께끼

"Whomever I touch, I send back to the earth from whence he came."

"You move me to pity--you are so weak on this Earth made of granite."

"Oh! I understand you very well," said the little prince. "But why do you always speak in riddles?"

그는 어린 왕자의 발목을 금발찌처럼 휘감았다. "내가 건드리기만 하면 누구나 자신이 태어난 땅으로 돌아가지." 뱀은 다시 말했다. "하지만 너는 순수하고 솔직하니까, 그리고 다른 별에서 왔으니까…." 어린 왕자는 대답하지 않았다. "널 보면 안쓰러운 마음이 들어. 화강암으로 된 이 지구에서 살아가기엔 너무 연약해." 뱀이 말했다. "내가 널 도와줄 수 있어. 만약 네 별이 너무 그립다면 내가…." "오, 무슨 말인지 잘 알겠어." 어린 왕자가 대답했다. "그런데 넌 어째서 계속 수수께끼처럼 말하니?" "난 그 모든 수수께끼를 풀 수 있거든." 뱀이 말했다. 둘은 침묵에 잠겼다.

The little prince crossed the desert and met with only one flower. It was a flower with three petals, a flower of no account at all.

"Good morning," said the little prince.

"Good morning," said the flower.

"Where are the men?" the little prince asked, politely.

The flower had once seen a caravan passing.

"Men?" she echoed. "I think there are six or seven of them in existence. I saw them, several years ago. But one never knows where to find them. The wind blows them away. They have no roots, and that makes their life very difficult."

"Goodbye," said the little prince.

"Goodbye," said the flower.

어휘 cross 가로지르다 petal 꽃잎 no account 쓸모 없는 politely 공손하게 caravan 상인 무리 pass 지나가다 existence 존재 root 뿌리

The little prince crossed the desert and met with only one flower.

"But one never knows where to find them."

"They have no roots, and that makes their life very difficult."

어린 왕자는 사막을 가로질렀지만, 꽃 한 송이밖에 만나지 못했다. 꽃잎이 세 장 달린 볼품없는 꽃이었다. "안녕." 어린 왕자가 말했다. "안녕." 꽃이 말했다. "사람들은 어디에 있니?" 어린 왕자가 공손하게 물었다. 꽃은 언젠가 상인 무리가 지나가는 모습을 본 적이 있다. "사람들?" 꽃이 말했다. "한 예닐곱쯤 되었던 것 같아. 몇 년 전에 보았지. 하지만 그들을 어디서 발견할 수 있을지는 모르겠어. 바람 따라 흘러 다니거든. 그들은 뿌리가 없어, 그것이 그들의 삶을 무척 힘들게 해." "잘 있어." 어린 왕자가 말했다. "잘 가." 꽃이 말했다.

After that, the little prince climbed a high mountain. The only mountains he had ever known were the three volcanoes, which came up to his knees. And he used the extinct volcano as a footstool. "From a mountain as high as this one," he said to himself, "I shall be able to see the whole planet at one glance, and all the people..."

But he saw nothing, save peaks of rock that were sharpened like needles.

어휘 climb 오르다 knee 무릎 footstool 발판 whole 전체 glance 훑어봄 peak 봉우리
needle 바늘

After that, the little prince climbed a high mountain.

"From a mountain as high as this one," he said to himself, "I shall be able to see the whole planet at one glance, and all the people..."

But he saw nothing, save peaks of rock that were sharpened like needles.

꽃과 작별한 후, 어린 왕자는 높은 산 위로 올라갔다. 그때까지 그가 알던 산이라곤 무릎 높이의 화산 세 개뿐이었다. 그는 사화산을 발판으로 사용하곤 했다. "이렇게 높은 산이라면," 그가 중얼거렸다. "이 별에 있는 모든 사람들을 한 번에 볼 수 있을 거야. 그러면 그들을⋯." 하지만 아무도 보이지 않았다. 그의 눈에 비친 거라곤 바늘 끝처럼 뾰족한 바위 봉우리들뿐이었다.

"Good morning," he said courteously.

"Good morning--Good morning--Good morning," answered the echo.

"Who are you?" said the little prince.

"Who are you--Who are you--Who are you?" answered the echo.

"Be my friends. I am all alone," he said.

"I am all alone--all alone--all alone," answered the echo.

"What a queer planet!" he thought. "It is altogether dry, and altogether pointed, and altogether harsh and forbidding. And the people have no imagination. They repeat whatever one says to them... On my planet I had a flower; she always was the first to speak..."

어휘 echo 메아리 alone 외로운 queer 이상한 altogether 전부 point 뾰족한 harsh 거친 forbidding 험악한, 무서운 imagination 상상력

"Good morning--Good morning--Good morning," answered the echo.

"What a queer planet!" he thought.

"It is altogether dry, and altogether pointed, and altogether harsh and forbidding."

"안녕." 그가 정중하게 인사했다. "안녕… 안녕… 안녕…." 메아리가 대답했다. "너는 누구니?" 어린 왕자가 물었다. "너는 누구니… 너는 누구니… 너는 누구니…?" 메아리가 대답했다. "내 친구가 되어 줘. 난 완전히 혼자야." 어린 왕자가 말했다. "혼자야… 혼자야… 혼자야…." 메아리가 대답했다. "참 이상한 별이야!" 그는 생각했다. "너무 건조하고 너무 뾰족한데다 거칠고 험악해. 게다가 사람들은 상상력이 없어. 다른 사람이 한 말을 반복하기만 하잖아. 내가 살던 별에는 꽃이 있었는데. 그 꽃은 언제나 먼저 말을 걸어 줬지…."

ut it happened that after walking for a long time through sand, and rocks, and snow, the little prince at last came upon a road. And all roads lead to the abodes of men.

"Good morning," he said.

He was standing before a garden, all a-bloom with roses.

"Good morning," said the roses.

The little prince gazed at them. They all looked like his flower.

"Who are you?" he demanded, thunderstruck.

"We are roses," the roses said.

And he was overcome with sadness. His flower had told him that she was the only one of her kind in all the universe. And here were five thousand of them, all alike, in one single garden!

 어휘   rock 바위   road 도로   abode 집, 거주지   demand 묻다   thunderstruck 깜짝 놀란
be overcome with 휩싸이다   sadness 슬픔   universe 우주   alike 비슷한

He was standing before a garden, all a-bloom with roses.

His flower had told him that she was the only one of her kind in all the universe.

And here were five thousand of them, all alike, in one single garden!

하지만 어린 왕자는 모래와 바위와 눈으로 덮인 길을 오랫동안 걸은 끝에 길 하나를 발견했다. 그 길은 사람들이 사는 곳으로 이어졌다. "안녕." 그가 말했다. 그는 장미가 만발한 정원 앞에 서 있었다. "안녕." 장미들이 말했다. 어린 왕자는 그들을 살펴보았다. 하나같이 그의 꽃과 닮아 있었다. "너희는 누구니?" 깜짝 놀란 어린 왕자가 물었다. "우린 장미야." 장미들이 대답했다. 어린 왕자는 슬픔에 사로잡혔다. 온 우주에 자기와 같은 꽃은 단 하나뿐이라고, 그의 꽃은 말했었다. 그런데 단 하나의 정원에 그와 꼭 닮은 꽃이 오천 송이나 피어 있다니!

"She would be very much annoyed," he said to himself, "if she should see that... She would cough most dreadfully, and she would pretend that she was dying, to avoid being laughed at. And I should be obliged to pretend that I was nursing her back to life--for if I did not do that, to humble myself also, she would really allow herself to die..."

Then he went on with his reflections: "I thought that I was rich, with a flower that was unique in all the world; and all I had was a common rose. A common rose, and three volcanoes that come up to my knees--and one of them perhaps extinct forever... That doesn't make me a very great prince..."

And he lay down in the grass and cried.

어휘 annoyed 화가 난 cough 기침하다 dreadfully 심하게 pretend ~인 척하다
avoid 피하다 be obliged to 하는 수 없이 ~하다 nurse 간호하다 humble 낮추다
reflection 생각

"She would be very much annoyed," he said to himself, "if she should see that…"

_____

_____

"I thought that I was rich, with a flower that was unique in all the world; and all I had was a common rose."

_____

_____

"That doesn't make me a very great prince…" And he lay down in the grass and cried.

_____

_____

"내 꽃이 이 광경을 보면 무척 화를 내겠는걸." 그가 중얼거렸다. "지독한 기침을 해대면서 창피한 모습을 숨기려고 죽어가는 척할 거야. 그럼 나는 그를 간호해서 살려내는 척해야겠지. 만약 그렇게 하지 않으면 나까지 창피하게 만들려고 진짜 죽어버릴지도 모르거든…." 그는 생각을 이어갔다. "내가 우주에 하나뿐인 꽃을 가진 부자인 줄 알았는데, 사실은 흔해 빠진 장미 한 송이를 갖고 있을 뿐이었구나. 흔해 빠진 장미에 무릎 높이까지 오는 화산 세 개…. 게다가 그중 하나는 아마도 영영 불을 뿜지 않을 테고…. 난 멋진 왕자가 아니었던 거야." 그는 풀밭에 몸을 넌 채 울었다.

I t was then that the fox appeared.

"Good morning," said the fox.

"Good morning," the little prince responded politely, although when he turned around he saw nothing.

"I am right here," the voice said, "under the apple tree."

"Who are you?" asked the little prince, and added, "You are very pretty to look at."

"I am a fox," the fox said.

"Come and play with me," proposed the little prince. "I am so unhappy."

여휘 fox 여우 appear 나타나다 respond 대답하다 politely 공손히 although 그러나 turn around 돌아보다 propose 제안하다 unhappy 불행한

It was then that the fox appeared.

"Who are you?" asked the little prince, and added, "You are very pretty to look at."

"Come and play with me," proposed the little prince. "I am so unhappy."

여우가 나타난 것은 그때였다. "안녕." 여우가 말했다. "안녕." 어린 왕자는 공손하게 대답하고 몸을 돌렸지만 아무도 보이지 않았다. "난 여기 있어." 목소리가 말했다. "사과나무 아래." "넌 누구니? 무척 예쁘구나." 어린 왕자가 물었다. "난 여우야." 여우가 말했다. "이리 와서 나랑 놀자." 어린 왕자가 청했다. "난 너무 슬퍼."

"I cannot play with you," the fox said. "I am not tamed."

"Ah! Please excuse me," said the little prince.

But, after some thought, he added:

"What does that mean--'tame'?"

"You do not live here," said the fox. "What is it that you are looking for?"

"I am looking for men," said the little prince. "What does that mean--'tame'?"

"Men," said the fox. "They have guns, and they hunt. It is very disturbing. They also raise chickens. These are their only interests. Are you looking for chickens?"

"No," said the little prince. "I am looking for friends. What does that mean--'tame'?"

"It is an act too often neglected," said the fox. "It means to establish ties."

" 'To establish ties'?"

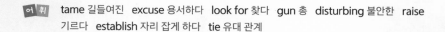

어휘   tame 길들여진   excuse 용서하다   look for 찾다   gun 총   disturbing 불안한   raise 기르다   establish 자리 잡게 하다   tie 유대 관계

I cannot play with you," the fox said. "I am not tamed."

"What does that mean-'tame'?"

"It is an act too often neglected," said the fox. "It means to establish ties."

"난 너랑 놀 수 없어." 여우가 말했다. "난 길들여지지 않았거든." "오, 미안해." 어린 왕자는 대답한 뒤 곰곰이 생각하다가 물었다. "그런데 '길들인다'는 건 뭐야?" "넌 이곳 사람이 아니구나." 여우가 말했다. "여기서 뭘 찾고 있니?" "난 사람을 찾고 있어. 그런데 '길들인다'는 게 뭐야?" "사람이라." 여우가 말했다. "사람들은 총을 가지고 사냥을 해. 그건 정말 난처한 일이야. 그들은 닭을 기르기도 해. 그게 그들의 유일한 관심사이지. 넌 닭을 찾고 있니?" "아니." 어린 왕자가 말했다. "난 친구들을 찾고 있어. 그런데 '길들인다'는 게 뭐야?" "너무 자주 잊히는 말이지. 그건 유대 관계를 맺는다는 뜻이야." "유대 관계를 맺는다고?"

"Just that," said the fox. "To me, you are still nothing more than a little boy who is just like a hundred thousand other little boys. And I have no need of you. And you, on your part, have no need of me. To you, I am nothing more than a fox like a hundred thousand other foxes. But if you tame me, then we shall need each other. To me, you will be unique in all the world. To you, I shall be unique in all the world..."

"I am beginning to understand," said the little prince. "There is a flower... I think that she has tamed me..."

"It is possible," said the fox. "On the Earth one sees all sorts of things."

"Oh, but this is not on the Earth!" said the little prince.

The fox seemed perplexed, and very curious.

"On another planet?"

"Yes."

---

 still 여전히 other 또 다른 need 필요로 하다 unique 유일한 perplexed 당황한
curious 호기심을 느끼는

"To me, you are still nothing more than a little boy who is just like a hundred thousand other little boys."

"But if you tame me, then we shall need each other."

"To me, you will be unique in all the world. To you, I shall be unique in all the world..."

"맞아." 여우가 말했다. "내게 너는 아직 수많은 다른 소년과 똑같은 한 명의 소년에 불과해. 난 네가 필요하지 않고, 너 또한 내가 필요하지 않지. 네게 난 수많은 다른 여우들과 똑같은 여우에 불과하니까. 하지만 네가 나를 길들인다면, 우린 서로를 필요로 하는 존재가 돼. 내게 넌 세상에서 유일한 존재가 되고, 나 또한 네게 세상에서 유일한 존재가 되는 거야…." "무슨 말인지 알 것 같아." 어린 왕자가 말했다. "꽃 한 송이가 있어…. 그 꽃이 날 길들인 것 같아…." "그럴 수 있지." 여우가 말했다. "지구에서는 별일이 다 일어나니까." "하지만 그건 지구에서 일어난 일이 아니야." 어린 왕자가 말했다. 여우는 혼란스러우면서도 큰 호기심을 느꼈다. "그럼 다른 별에서 있었던 일이야?" "맞아."

"Are there hunters on that planet?"

"No."

"Ah, that is interesting! Are there chickens?"

"No."

"Nothing is perfect," sighed the fox.

But he came back to his idea.

"My life is very monotonous," the fox said. "I hunt chickens; men hunt me.

All the chickens are just alike, and all the men are just alike.

어휘 hunter 사냥꾼 interesting 흥미로운 perfect 완벽한 sigh 한숨 쉬다 monotonous 단조로운 hunt 사냥하다 alike 비슷한

"Nothing is perfect," sighed the fox.

"My life is very monotonous," the fox said. "I hunt chickens; men hunt me."

"All the chickens are just alike, and all the men are just alike."

"그 별에도 사냥꾼들이 있니?" "아니." "그것 참 흥미로운걸! 그럼 닭은?" "없어." "세상에 완벽한 것은 없지." 여우는 한숨을 내쉬었다. 하지만 곧 이야기를 계속했다. "내 삶은 굉장히 단조로워. 나는 닭을 쫓고 사람들은 나를 쫓아. 닭들은 모두 똑같고 사람들도 마찬가지야.

And, in consequence, I am a little bored. But if you tame me, it will be as if the sun came to shine on my life. I shall know the sound of a step that will be different from all the others. Other steps send me hurrying back underneath the ground. Yours will call me, like music, out of my burrow. And then look: you see the grain-fields down yonder? I do not eat bread. Wheat is of no use to me. The wheat fields have nothing to say to me. And that is sad. But you have hair that is the color of gold. Think how wonderful that will be when you have tamed me! The grain, which is also golden, will bring me back the thought of you. And I shall love to listen to the wind in the wheat..."

The fox gazed at the little prince, for a long time.

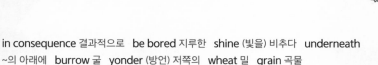

어휘 in consequence 결과적으로 be bored 지루한 shine (빛을) 비추다 underneath ~의 아래에 burrow 굴 yonder (방언) 저쪽의 wheat 밀 grain 곡물

"But if you tame me, it will be as if the sun came to shine on my life."

"I shall know the sound of a step that will be different from all the others."

"And I shall love to listen to the wind in the wheat..."

그래서 난 조금 지루해. 하지만 네가 날 길들인다면 내 삶에는 환한 햇살이 비출 거야. 나는 다른 발소리들과 네 발소리를 구분하게 되겠지. 다른 발소리는 나를 땅속으로 숨게 만들지만, 네 발소리는 마치 음악처럼 나를 굴 밖으로 부를 거야. 그리고 저길 봐. 저쪽에 있는 밀밭이 보이지? 난 빵을 먹지 않아. 저 밭은 내게 아무 소용이 없어. 밀밭은 내게 아무 의미도 주지 못하지. 그건 슬픈 일이야. 하지만 넌 금빛 머리칼을 가졌고, 네가 나를 길들인다면 정말 놀라운 일이 일어날 거야! 밀은 네 머리칼과 닮은 금빛이니까, 나는 밀을 보며 너를 떠올릴 수 있어. 나는 밀밭에 부는 바람 소리마저 사랑하게 될 거야…" 여우는 어린 왕자를 한참 동안 바라보았다.

"Please--tame me!" he said.

"I want to, very much," the little prince replied. "But I have not much time. I have friends to discover, and a great many things to understand."

"One only understands the things that one tames," said the fox. "Men have no more time to understand anything. They buy things all ready made at the shops. But there is no shop anywhere where one can buy friendship, and so men have no friends any more. If you want a friend, tame me..."

"What must I do, to tame you?" asked the little prince.

"You must be very patient," replied the fox. "First you will sit down at a little distance from me--like that--in the grass. I shall look at you out of the corner of my eye, and you will say nothing. Words are the source of misunderstandings. But you will sit a little closer to me, every day..."

The next day the little prince came back.

어휘 discover 발견하다 understand 이해하다 friendship 우정 patient 인내심
distance 거리 source 원천 misunderstanding 오해

"One only understands the things that one tames," said the fox.

"What must I do, to tame you?" asked the little prince.

"But you will sit a little closer to me, every day…"

"나를… 길들여 줘!" 여우가 말했다. "나도 그러고 싶어. 정말이야." 어린 왕자가 대답했다. "하지만 내게는 시간이 없어. 난 친구들을 발견해야 하고, 알아야 할 것들도 많아." "우리는 직접 길들인 것 말고는 알 수 없어." 여우가 말했다. "사람들은 이제 아무것도 알 시간이 없지. 이미 만들어진 물건들을 상점에서 살 뿐이니까. 하지만 우정을 파는 상점은 없거든. 그러니 사람들은 더 이상 친구를 만들지 못해. 네가 원하는 게 친구라면 나를 길들여 줘…." "널 길들이려면 어떻게 해야 하는데?" 어린 왕자가 물었다. "인내심을 가져야 해." 여우가 대답했다. "처음에는 내게서 조금 멀리 떨어져 있어. 바로 그렇게, 풀밭에 앉아 있는 거야. 난 너를 곁눈질로 지켜보겠지. 너는 말없이 있어야 해. 말은 모든 오해의 근원이니까. 하지만 매일 조금씩 내게 다가오는 거야." 다음 날 어린 왕자는 다시 그곳으로 갔다.

"It would have been better to come back at the same hour," said the fox. "If, for example, you come at four o'clock in the afternoon, then at three o'clock I shall begin to be happy. I shall feel happier and happier as the hour advances. At four o'clock, I shall already be worrying and jumping about. I shall show you how happy I am! But if you come at just any time, I shall never know at what hour my heart is to be ready to greet you... One must observe the proper rites..."

"What is a rite?" asked the little prince.

"Those also are actions too often neglected," said the fox. "They are what make one day different from other days, one hour from other hours. There is a rite, for example, among my hunters. Every Thursday they dance with the village girls. So Thursday is a wonderful day for me! I can take a walk as far as the vineyards. But if the hunters danced at just any time, every day would be like every other day, and I should never have any vacation at all."

어휘   advance 다가가다   worry 걱정하다   observe 지키다   proper 적절한   rite 의식
neglect 무시하다   village 마을   vineyard 포도밭

"If, for example, you come at four o'clock in the afternoon, then at three o'clock I shall begin to be happy."

"But if the hunters danced at just any time, every day would be like every other day, and I should never have any vacation at all."

"늘 같은 시간에 오면 더 좋아." 여우가 말했다. "만약 네가 오후 네 시에 온다면 난 세 시부터 행복해지기 시작할 거야. 행복은 시간이 갈수록 더 커져. 네 시가 되면 벌써 흥분해서 뛰어다니겠지. 내가 얼마나 행복한지 내게 보여 줄 수도 있을 거야. 하지만 네가 아무 때나 찾아온다면 언제부터 마음의 준비를 해야 할지 알 수 없잖아…. 그래서 우리에겐 적절한 의식이 필요한 거야." "의식이 뭐야?" 어린 왕자가 물었다. "그것 역시 너무 자주 잊히는 말이지." 여우가 말했다. "의식이란 어떤 날을 다른 날과 다르게 만들고, 어떤 시간을 다른 시간과 다르게 만드는 거야. 예를 들어, 나를 쫓는 사냥꾼들에게는 매주 목요일에 마을 처녀들과 춤을 춘다는 의식이 있어. 그러니 목요일은 내게 멋진 날이지! 그날은 포도밭까지 나가서 산책을 할 수 있거든. 하지만 사냥꾼들이 아무 때나 춤을 춘다면, 매일이 다른 날과 다를 바 없는 똑같은 하루일 거야. 그럼 내겐 휴가가 없겠지."

So the little prince tamed the fox. And when the hour of his departure drew near--

"Ah," said the fox, "I shall cry."

"It is your own fault," said the little prince. "I never wished you any sort of harm; but you wanted me to tame you..."

"Yes, that is so," said the fox.

"But now you are going to cry!" said the little prince.

"Yes, that is so," said the fox.

"Then it has done you no good at all!"

"It has done me good," said the fox, "because of the color of the wheat fields." And then he added:

"Go and look again at the roses. You will understand now that yours is unique in all the world. Then come back to say goodbye to me, and I will make you a present of a secret."

The little prince went away, to look again at the roses.

어휘 departure 떠남 draw near 다가오다, 접근하다 wish 바라다 harm 해악 wheat field 밀밭 present 말하다, 설명하다 secret 비밀

So the little prince tamed the fox.

"It is your own fault," said the little prince. "I never wished you any sort of harm; but you wanted me to tame you…"

"Go and look again at the roses. You will understand now that yours is unique in all the world."

어린 왕자는 그렇게 여우를 길들였다. 이별의 시간이 다가왔을 때, 여우가 말했다. "아, 나 울 것 같아." "그건 네 잘못이야." 어린 왕자가 말했다. "난 네게 아무런 해를 끼치고 싶지 않았어. 하지만 네가 길들여 달라고 했잖아…." "그래, 네 말이 맞아." 여우가 말했다. "하지만 너 지금 울려고 하잖아!" 어린 왕자가 말했다. "그래, 네 말이 맞아." 여우가 말했다. "그러면 결국 너에게 좋은 게 전혀 없었네!" "좋은 거 있었어." 여우가 말했다. "밀밭의 색이 있잖아." 그리고 말을 덧붙였다. "가서 장미꽃들을 다시 봐. 네 꽃이 세상에서 유일한 존재라는 사실을 알게 될 거야. 그런 다음 돌아와서 내게 작별 인사를 해 주렴. 그러면 선물로 네게 비밀 하나를 알려 줄게." 어린 왕자는 여우를 떠나 장미들을 다시 보러 갔다.

"You are not at all like my rose," he said. "As yet you are nothing. No one has tamed you, and you have tamed no one. You are like my fox when I first knew him. He was only a fox like a hundred thousand other foxes. But I have made him my friend, and now he is unique in all the world."

And the roses were very much embarrassed.

"You are beautiful, but you are empty," he went on. "One could not die for you. To be sure, an ordinary passerby would think that my rose looked just like you--the rose that belongs to me. But in herself alone she is more important than all the hundreds of you other roses: because it is she that I have watered; because it is she that I have put under the glass globe; because it is she that I have sheltered behind the screen; because it is for her that I have killed the caterpillars (except the two or three that we saved to become butterflies); because it is she that I have listened to, when she grumbled, or boasted, or ever sometimes when she said nothing. Because she is *my* rose.

어휘 as yet 아직 empty 텅 빈 ordinary 평범한 passerby 행인 water 물을 주다
shelter (비 바람을) 막아주다 caterpillar 애벌레 except ~를 제외하고
grumble 투덜거리다 boast 뽐내다

"You are not at all like my rose," he said.

"To be sure, an ordinary passerby would think that my rose looked just like you--the rose that belongs to me."

"But in herself alone she is more important than all the hundreds of you other roses."

해석

"너희는 내 꽃과 전혀 닮지 않았어." 어린 왕자가 말했다. "너희는 아직 아무것도 아니야. 아무도 너희를 길들이지 않았고, 너희도 누군가를 길들이지 않았으니까. 너희는 예전의 내 여우와 같아. 그는 수많은 다른 여우들과 똑같은 여우에 불과했지. 하지만 난 그를 친구로 만들었고, 이제 그는 세상에서 유일한 존재야." 장미들은 그의 말에 당황했다. "너희는 아름답지만 텅 비어 있어." 어린 왕자가 말을 이었다. "너희를 위해 죽을 수 있는 사람은 없겠지. 물론 지나가던 사람에겐 내 꽃이 너희와 다를 바 없어 보일 거야. 그저 내가 가진 장미라고만 생각하겠지. 하지만 내게 그 꽃은 너희와 같은 장미 수백 송이보다 훨씬 중요해. 내가 그 꽃에 물을 주었으니까. 내가 유리 덮개를 씌워 주었고, 내가 바람막이로 보호해 주었으니까. 나는 그 꽃을 위해 애벌레도 잡아 주었어(두세 마리 정도는 나비가 되라고 남겨 두었지만). 불평할 때도, 허세를 부릴 때도, 심지어 침묵할 때조차 그에게 귀를 기울였던 건 오직 그녀가 '나의' 꽃이기 때문이야."

And he went back to meet the fox.

"Goodbye," he said.

"Goodbye," said the fox. "And now here is my secret, a very simple secret: It is only with the heart that one can see rightly; what is essential is invisible to the eye."

"What is essential is invisible to the eye," the little prince repeated, so that he would be sure to remember.

"It is the time you have wasted for your rose that makes your rose so important."

"It is the time I have wasted for my rose--" said the little prince, so that he would be sure to remember.

"Men have forgotten this truth," said the fox. "But you must not forget it. You become responsible, forever, for what you have tamed. You are responsible for your rose..."

"I am responsible for my rose," the little prince repeated, so that he would be sure to remember.

어휘 secret 비밀 rightly 제대로 essential 중요한 invisible 보이지 않는 repeat 반복하다 waste 낭비하다 be responsible for ~에 책임이 있다

"It is only with the heart that one can see rightly; what is essential is invisible to the eye."

"It is the time you have wasted for your rose that makes your rose so important."

"I am responsible for my rose."

 해 석

그리고 어린 왕자는 여우를 만나기 위해 돌아왔다. "잘 있어." 어린 왕자가 말했다. "잘 가." 여우가 말했다. "내 비밀을 알려 줄게. 아주 간단해. 제대로 보려면 마음으로 보아야 해. 중요한 것은 눈에 보이지 않거든." "중요한 건 눈에 보이지 않는다." 어린 왕자는 확실히 기억하려고 그 말을 되풀이했다. "네 장미를 그토록 소중하게 만든 건 네가 그 꽃을 위해 쏟은 시간이야." "꽃을 위해 쏟은 시간…." 어린 왕자는 확실히 기억하려고 그 말을 되풀이했다. "사람들은 이 진리를 잊어버렸지." 여우가 말했다. "하지만 넌 잊지 마. 너는 네가 길들인 것에 언제까지나 책임이 있어. 너는 네 장미에 책임이 있는 거야…." "나는 내 장미에 책임이 있어." 어린 왕자는 확실히 기억하려고 그 말을 되풀이했다.

"**G**ood morning," said the little prince.

"Good morning," said the railway switchman.

"What do you do here?" the little prince asked.

"I sort out travelers, in bundles of a thousand," said the switchman. "I send off the trains that carry them: now to the right, now to the left."

And a brilliantly lighted express train shook the switchman's cabin as it rushed by with a roar like thunder.

"They are in a great hurry," said the little prince. "What are they looking for?"

"Not even the locomotive engineer knows that," said the switchman.

And a second brilliantly lighted express thundered by, in the opposite direction.

"Are they coming back already?" demanded the little prince.

"These are not the same ones," said the switchman. "It is an exchange."

어휘 railway switchman 철도 교환원 bundle 묶음, 무리 send off 배웅하다, 전송하다
carry 실어 나르다 express 급행열차 cabin (철도의) 신호소 locomotive 기관차
opposite 반대의 direction 방향 exchange 교환

"I send off the trains that carry them: now to the right, now to the left."

"They are in a great hurry," said the little prince. "What are they looking for?"

"Not even the locomotive engineer knows that," said the switchman.

해석

"안녕하세요." 어린 왕자가 말했다. "안녕." 철도 교환원이 말했다. "여기서 뭘 하고 계세요?" 어린 왕자가 물었다. "이동하는 사람들을 분류하지. 천 명씩 한 묶음으로 솎는 거야." 교환원이 말했다. "그리고 그들이 탄 기차를 오른쪽으로 보내거나 왼쪽으로 보낸단다." 그때 환하게 불을 밝힌 급행열차 한 대가 천둥처럼 다가와 교환원의 사무실을 뒤흔들며 지나갔다. "저 사람들은 무척 바쁜가 봐요." 어린 왕자가 말했다. "저들은 무엇을 찾고 있나요?" "저들을 싣고 가는 기관사도 모른단다." 교환원이 대답했다. 반대 방향에서 불을 밝힌 또 다른 급행열차가 요란한 소리를 내며 지나갔다. "아까 갔던 사람들이 벌써 돌아오는 건가요?" 어린 왕자가 물었다. "아까 그 사람들이 아니야." 교환원이 말했다. "서로 엇갈려 반대로 가는 거지."

"Were they not satisfied where they were?" asked the little prince.

"No one is ever satisfied where he is," said the switchman.

And they heard the roaring thunder of a third brilliantly lighted express.

"Are they pursuing the first travelers?" demanded the little prince.

"They are pursuing nothing at all," said the switchman. "They are asleep in there, or if they are not asleep they are yawning. Only the children are flattening their noses against the windowpanes."

"Only the children know what they are looking for," said the little prince. "They waste their time over a rag doll and it becomes very important to them; and if anybody takes it away from them, they cry..."

"They are lucky," the switchman said.

어휘   satisfy 만족하다   roar 으르렁대다   thunder 천둥 (소리)   pursue 쫓다
asleep 잠이 든   flatten 납작하게 만들다   windowpane 창유리   rag 해진 천

"No one is ever satisfied where he is," said the switchman.

_____

_____

"Only the children are flattening their noses against the windowpanes."

_____

_____

"Only the children know what they are looking for," said the little prince.

_____

_____

"원래 살던 곳에 만족하지 못해서요?" 어린 왕자가 물었다. "원래 살던 곳에 만족하는 사람은 없어." 교환원이 대답했다. 불을 밝힌 세 번째 급행열차가 천둥 같은 소리를 울렸다. "저들은 처음에 지나간 사람들을 쫓아가는 건가요?" 어린 왕자가 물었다. "저들은 아무것도 쫓지 않아." 교환원이 말했다. "기차 안에서 잠을 자거나 하품을 하고 있을 거다. 어린아이들이나 창문에 코를 납작하게 붙이고 있지." "어린이들만 자신이 무엇을 찾는지 알고 있어요." 어린 왕자가 말했다. "그들은 낡은 인형에 시간을 쏟고, 그 인형은 그들에게 아주 중요한 것이 돼요. 누군가 그걸 빼앗아 가면 울음을 터뜨리죠…." "아이들은 운이 좋지." 교환원이 말했다.

"Good morning," said the little prince.

"Good morning," said the merchant.

This was a merchant who sold pills that had been invented to quench thirst. You need only swallow one pill a week, and you would feel no need of anything to drink.

"Why are you selling those?" asked the little prince.

"Because they save a tremendous amount of time," said the merchant. "Computations have been made by experts. With these pills, you save fifty-three minutes in every week."

"And what do I do with those fifty-three minutes?"

"Anything you like..."

"As for me," said the little prince to himself, "if I had fifty-three minutes to spend as I liked, I should walk at my leisure toward a spring of fresh water."

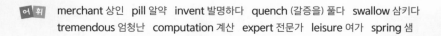

어휘 merchant 상인 pill 알약 invent 발명하다 quench (갈증을) 풀다 swallow 삼키다
tremendous 엄청난 computation 계산 expert 전문가 leisure 여가 spring 샘

This was a merchant who sold pills that had been invented to quench thirst.

"Computations have been made by experts. With these pills, you save fifty-three minutes in every week."

"If I had fifty-three minutes to spend as I liked, I should walk at my leisure toward a spring of fresh water."

"안녕하세요." 어린 왕자가 말했다. "안녕." 장사꾼이 말했다. 장사꾼은 얼마 전 개발되었다는, 갈증을 풀어 준다는 알약을 판매하고 있었다. 일주일에 한 알만 먹으면 마시고 싶다는 욕망을 느끼지 않는다는 것이다. "왜 이런 걸 팔아요?" 어린 왕자가 물었다. "시간을 엄청나게 절약해 주거든." 장사꾼이 말했다. "전문가들이 계산을 해 봤는데, 이 약을 먹으면 매주 오십삼 분씩 절약할 수 있단다." "그럼 그 오십삼 분으로 뭘 하는데요?" "원하는 걸 뭐든 할 수 있지." "만약 내게 자유롭게 쓸 수 있는 오십삼 분이 생긴다면," 어린 왕자가 중얼거렸다. "맑은 물이 솟는 샘까지 느긋하게 걸어갈 텐데."

It was now the eighth day since I had had my accident in the desert, and I had listened to the story of the merchant as I was drinking the last drop of my water supply.

"Ah," I said to the little prince, "these memories of yours are very charming; but I have not yet succeeded in repairing my plane; I have nothing more to drink; and I, too, should be very happy if I could walk at my leisure toward a spring of fresh water!"

"My friend the fox--" the little prince said to me.

"My dear little man, this is no longer a matter that has anything to do with the fox!"

"Why not?"

"Because I am about to die of thirst..."

He did not follow my reasoning, and he answered me:

"It is a good thing to have had a friend, even if one is about to die. I, for instance, am very glad to have had a fox as a friend..."

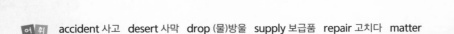

어휘 accident 사고 desert 사막 drop (물)방울 supply 보급품 repair 고치다 matter 중요한 reasoning 추론, 사고

I had listened to the story of the merchant as I was drinking the last drop of my water supply.

"Because I am about to die of thirst…"

"It is a good thing to have had a friend, even if one is about to die."

사막에서 비행기가 고장이 난 지 여드레째 되는 날이었다. 나는 마지막 남은 물을 마시며 장사꾼 이야기를 들었다. 나는 어린 왕자에게 말했다. "아, 네 추억은 정말 아름답구나. 하지만 난 아직 비행기를 고치지 못했어. 이제 남은 물도 없지. 맑은 물이 솟는 샘까지 느긋하게 걸어갈 수 있다면 나도 정말 행복하겠다!" "내 친구 여우는…." 어린 왕자가 말했다. "꼬마 친구, 이제 여우 이야기 같은 건 아무 의미가 없어!" "어째서?" "목이 말라 죽겠으니까…." 그는 내 말을 이해하지 못한 채 이렇게 대답했다. "죽을 것 같은 순간이라 해도 친구가 있다는 건 좋은 일이야. 난 여우가 내 친구라서 정말 기쁘고…."

"He has no way of guessing the danger," I said to myself. "He has never been either hungry or thirsty. A little sunshine is all he needs..."

But he looked at me steadily, and replied to my thought:

"I am thirsty, too. Let us look for a well..."

I made a gesture of weariness. It is absurd to look for a well, at random, in the immensity of the desert. But nevertheless we started walking.

When we had trudged along for several hours, in silence, the darkness fell, and the stars began to come out. Thirst had made me a little feverish, and I looked at them as if I were in a dream. The little prince's last words came reeling back into my memory:

"Then you are thirsty, too?" I demanded.

But he did not reply to my question. He merely said to me:

"Water may also be good for the heart..."

---

 steadily 계속, 꾸준히 well 우물 weariness 피로함 absurd 어리석은 at random 되는 대로 immensity 광활한 공간 trudge 터덜터덜 걷다 feverish 열이 오른 reel 빙빙 돌다 merely 그저, 단지

"A little sunshine is all he needs…"

_____

_____

When we had trudged along for several hours, in silence, the darkness fell, and the stars began to come out.

_____

_____

"Water may also be good for the heart…"

_____

_____

 해 석

"이 아이는 위험을 전혀 감지할 줄 모르는군." 나는 중얼거렸다. "배고픔이나 목마름을 느껴 본 적 없는 거야. 햇빛 조금만 있으면 그걸로 충분하니까…." 하지만 그는 나를 빤히 바라보더니 내 생각에 응답하듯 말했다. "나도 목말라. 우리 샘을 찾으러 가자." 나는 피곤하다는 몸짓을 보였다. 이 광활한 사막에서 단서도 없이 샘을 찾는다는 건 바보 같은 짓이었다. 그러나 어쨌든 우리는 걷기 시작했다. 침묵 속에서 몇 시간쯤 걸었을까. 어둠이 내리고 별이 반짝이기 시작했다. 갈증 때문에 열이 조금 있던 내게 그 별들은 마치 꿈속의 한 장면처럼 보였다. 어린 왕자가 한 말들이 머릿속을 맴돌았다. "너도 목마르다고?" 내가 물었다. 그는 내 질문에 대답하는 대신 이렇게 말했다. "물은 마음에도 좋은걸…."

I did not understand this answer, but I said nothing. I knew very well that it was impossible to cross-examine him.

He was tired. He sat down. I sat down beside him. And, after a little silence, he spoke again:

"The stars are beautiful, because of a flower that cannot be seen."

I replied, "Yes, that is so." And, without saying anything more, I looked across the ridges of sand that were stretched out before us in the moonlight.

"The desert is beautiful," the little prince added.

And that was true. I have always loved the desert. One sits down on a desert sand dune, sees nothing, hears nothing. Yet through the silence something throbs, and gleams...

"What makes the desert beautiful," said the little prince, "is that somewhere it hides a well..."

어휘 cross-examine 반문하다 beside ~의 옆에 ridge 능선 stretch 뻗다 dune 모래 언덕 silence 침묵 throb (소리가) 울리다 gleam 빛남 hide 숨기다

I did not understand this answer, but I said nothing.

"The stars are beautiful, because of a flower that cannot be seen.

"What makes the desert beautiful," said the little prince, "is that somewhere it hides a well..."

나는 그의 대답을 이해하지 못했으나, 아무 말도 하지 않았다. 그에게 반문하는 것은 불가능하다는 것을 잘 알았기 때문이다. 그는 지쳐 있었다. 그가 땅바닥에 앉았다. 나는 그의 옆에 자리를 잡았다. 잠시 침묵을 지키던 그가 다시 말을 이었다. "별들이 아름다운 건 보이지 않는 꽃 한 송이가 있기 때문이야." "맞아, 그렇지." 나는 대답했다. 그리고 말없이 달빛 아래 펼쳐진 모래 언덕의 능선들을 바라보았다. "사막은 아름다워." 어린 왕자가 덧붙였다. 그 말은 사실이었다. 나는 언제나 사막을 사랑했다. 사막의 모래 언덕에 앉으면 아무것도 보이지 않고 아무것도 들리지 않는다. 그러나 고요 속에서 울리고 빛나는 무언가가 있다…. "사막이 아름다운 건." 어린 왕자가 말했다. "어딘가에 샘을 숨기고 있기 때문이야…."

I was astonished by a sudden understanding of that mysterious radiation of the sands. When I was a little boy I lived in an old house, and legend told us that a treasure was buried there. To be sure, no one had ever known how to find it; perhaps no one had ever even looked for it. But it cast an enchantment over that house. My home was hiding a secret in the depths of its heart...

"Yes," I said to the little prince. "The house, the stars, the desert--what gives them their beauty is something that is invisible!"

"I am glad," he said, "that you agree with my fox."

어휘 astonish 깜짝 놀라게 하다 sudden 갑작스러운 mysterious 신비한 radiation 빛
treasure 보물 bury 묻다 enchantment 매혹, 매력 depth 깊은 곳

I was astonished by a sudden understanding of that mysterious radiation of the sands.

When I was a little boy I lived in an old house, and legend told us that a treasure was buried there.

My home was hiding a secret in the depths of its heart...

그 순간 나는 사막의 모래가 퍼뜨리는 신비로운 빛이 무엇인지 깨닫고 깜짝 놀랐다. 어린 시절, 내가 살던 오래된 집에는 보물이 묻혀 있다는 전설이 있었다. 물론 보물을 발견한 사람은 없었고, 어쩌면 실제로 찾아 본 사람도 없었을 것이다. 그럼에도 그 이야기는 집 전체에 매력을 더했다. 우리 집은 가장 깊숙한 곳에 보물을 감추고 있었던 것이다⋯. "맞아." 나는 어린 왕자에게 말했다. "집이든, 별이든, 사막이든, 그것들을 아름답게 하는 건 눈에 보이지 않는 무언가야." "아저씨가 내 여우와 같은 생각을 하고 있어서 기뻐." 그가 말했다.

The Little Prince
24

As the little prince dropped off to sleep, I took him in my arms and set out walking once more. I felt deeply moved, and stirred. It seemed to me that I was carrying a very fragile treasure. It seemed to me, even, that there was nothing more fragile on all Earth. In the moonlight I looked at his pale forehead, his closed eyes, his locks of hair that trembled in the wind, and I said to myself: "What I see here is nothing but a shell. What is most important is invisible..."

As his lips opened slightly with the suspicion of a half-smile, I said to myself, again: "What moves me so deeply, about this little prince who is sleeping here, is his loyalty to a flower--the image of a rose that shines through his whole being like the flame of a lamp, even when he is asleep..." And I felt him to be more fragile still. I felt the need of protecting him, as if he himself were a flame that might be extinguished by a little puff of wind...

And, as I walked on so, I found the well, at daybreak.

어휘 drop off 깜빡 잠이 들다 stir 동요하다 fragile 깨지기 쉬운 tremble 떨리다 shell 껍데기 loyalty 충성심 shine 빛나다 flame 불꽃 extinguish (불을) 끄다 puff of wind 한 줄기 바람 daybreak 동틀 무렵

226

As the little prince dropped off to sleep, I took him in my arms and set out walking once more.

It seemed to me that I was carrying a very fragile treasure.

I felt the need of protecting him, as if he himself were a flame that might be extinguished by a little puff of wind...

어린 왕자는 잠이 들었고, 나는 그를 안아 든 채 다시 걷기 시작했다. 감동적이고 뭉클한 감정이 밀려왔다. 부서지기 쉬운 보물을 안고 가는 기분이었다. 그의 몸은 이 지구에서 가장 연약한 존재처럼 느껴졌다. 달빛에 비친 창백한 이마와 감긴 눈, 바람에 흩날리는 머리칼을 바라보며 나는 중얼거렸다. "내가 보는 건 그의 껍질에 지나지 않아. 진짜 중요한 건 보이지 않으니까⋯." 그의 살짝 열린 입술이 희미하게 미소 짓는 듯해서, 나는 또다시 중얼거렸다. "내 품에서 잠든 어린 왕자가 내 마음을 이토록 깊이 움직이는 건, 그가 꽃 한 송이에 바친 순정 때문일 거야. 그 꽃이 잠들어 있을 때조차 가로등 불빛처럼 그의 존재를 비춰주는 거지." 그러자 그가 더욱 부서지기 쉬운 존재처럼 느껴졌다. 나는 그를 보호해야 한다고 생각했다. 마치 그가 약한 바람 한 줄기에도 꺼질 수 있는 불꽃인 것처럼⋯. 그렇게 걷던 나는 동이 틀 무렵 샘을 발견했다.

"Men," said the little prince, "set out on their way in express trains, but they do not know what they are looking for. Then they rush about, and get excited, and turn round and round..."

And he added:

"It is not worth the trouble..."

The well that we had come to was not like the wells of the Sahara. The wells of the Sahara are mere holes dug in the sand. This one was like a well in a village. But there was no village here, and I thought I must be dreaming...

"It is strange," I said to the little prince. "Everything is ready for use: the pulley, the bucket, the rope..."

He laughed, touched the rope, and set the pulley to working. And the pulley moaned, like an old weathervane which the wind has long since forgotten.

어휘 rush 서두르다 get excited 흥분하다 worth ~할 가치가 있는 hole 구멍 village 마을 pulley 도르래 rope 밧줄 moan (바람의) 울리는 소리 weathervane 풍향계

"Men," said the little prince, "set out on their way in express trains, but they do not know what they are looking for."

"It is strange," I said to the little prince. "Everything is ready for use: the pulley, the bucket, the rope..."

He laughed, touched the rope, and set the pulley to working.

"사람들은 급행열차에 타지만." 어린 왕자가 말했다. "자신이 무엇을 찾고 있는지 몰라. 그래서 붕 뜨고 허둥지둥하며 같은 자리를 빙빙 도는 거야…." 그리고 이렇게 덧붙였다. "그럴 가치가 없는데…." 우리가 도달한 샘은 사하라 사막의 샘과는 달랐다. 사하라의 샘은 그저 모래에 파놓은 구덩이 같았지만, 이것은 마을에 있는 우물과 꽤 흡사했다. 그러나 그곳엔 마을이 없었다. 나는 꿈을 꾸는 기분이 들었다. "이상해." 내가 어린 왕자에게 말했다. "도르래며 양동이며 밧줄이며… 모든 게 갖춰져 있잖아." 그는 웃으며 밧줄을 잡고 도르래를 움직였다. 그러자 도르래는 오랜만에 바람을 맞은 낡은 풍향계처럼 삐그덕거렸다.

"Do you hear?" said the little prince. "We have wakened the well, and it is singing…"

I did not want him to tire himself with the rope.

"Leave it to me," I said. "It is too heavy for you."

I hoisted the bucket slowly to the edge of the well and set it there--happy, tired as I was, over my achievement. The song of the pulley was still in my ears, and I could see the sunlight shimmer in the still trembling water.

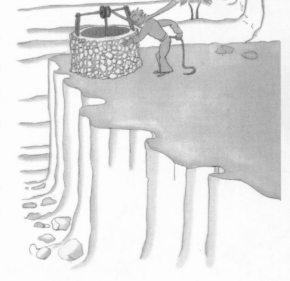

"I am thirsty for this water," said the little prince. "Give me some of it to drink…"

And I understood what he had been looking for.

---

 wake 깨우다 rope 밧줄 hoist 들어 올리다 edge 가장자리 achievement 성취
shimmer (빛이) 가물거리다 tremble 떨다

"Do you hear?" said the little prince. "We have wakened the well, and it is singing..."

I hoisted the bucket slowly to the edge of the well and set it there--happy, tired as I was, over my achievement.

And I understood what he had been looking for.

"들리지?" 어린 왕자가 말했다. "우리가 우물을 깨우니까 우물이 노래하잖아…." 나는 어린 왕자에게 물을 긷게 하고 싶지 않았다. "내가 할게. 너한텐 너무 무거워." 나는 우물 입구의 돌까지 바구니를 천천히 끌어 올려 고정시켰다. 스스로 해낸 성취에 피곤하면서도 행복한 기분이 들었다. 귀에는 여전히 도르래의 노랫소리가 울렸고, 여전히 출렁이는 물속에서 햇살이 일렁이고 있었다. "이 물을 마시고 싶어." 어린 왕자가 말했다. "내게 물을 줄래?" 나는 어린 왕자가 무엇을 찾고 있는지 이해했다.

I raised the bucket to his lips. He drank, his eyes closed. It was as sweet as some special festival treat. This water was indeed a different thing from ordinary nourishment. Its sweetness was born of the walk under the stars, the song of the pulley, the effort of my arms. It was good for the heart, like a present. When I was a little boy, the lights of the Christmas tree, the music of the Midnight Mass, the tenderness of smiling faces, used to make up, so, the radiance of the gifts I received.

"The men where you live," said the little prince, "raise five thousand roses in the same garden--and they do not find in it what they are looking for."

"They do not find it," I replied.

"And yet what they are looking for could be found in one single rose, or in a little water."

"Yes, that is true," I said.

And the little prince added:

"But the eyes are blind. One must look with the heart..."

어휘 lip 입술 indeed 참으로 nourishment 음식물 effort 노력 tenderness 부드러움
radiance 빛 receive 받다 find 찾다

This water was indeed a different thing from ordinary nourishment.

_____

_____

Its sweetness was born of the walk under the stars, the song of the pulley, the effort of my arms.

_____

_____

"And yet what they are looking for could be found in one single rose, or in a little water."

_____

_____

양동이를 그의 입술 가까이 가져가자, 그는 눈을 감고 물을 마셨다. 물에서는 특별한 축제와도 같은 달콤한 맛이 났다. 그 물은 일반적인 마실 것과 달랐다. 그것은 별빛 아래서의 여정과 도르래의 노래와 내 두 팔의 노력으로 얻어낸 보상이었다. 선물처럼 마음을 풍요롭게 만드는 것이었다. 어린 소년이었을 때는 크리스마스트리의 불빛과 자정 미사의 음악과 사람들의 얼굴에 어린 부드러운 미소가 내가 받은 선물들을 빛나게 만들어 주었다. "아저씨 별의 사람들은 정원 하나에 장미를 오천 송이나 키워." 어린 왕자가 말했다. "하지만 그 정원에서 자신이 무엇을 찾고 있는지는 몰라." "맞아, 모르지." 내가 대답했다. "하지만 그들이 찾는 것은 단 한 송이의 꽃이나 약간의 물에서 발견될 수도 있어." "맞아, 정말 그래." 내가 말했다. 어린 왕자가 덧붙였다. "하지만 눈으로는 볼 수 없어. 마음으로 보아야 해."

I had drunk the water. I breathed easily. At sunrise the sand is the color of honey. And that honey color was making me happy, too. What brought me, then, this sense of grief?

"You must keep your promise," said the little prince, softly, as he sat down beside me once more.

"What promise?"

"You know--a muzzle for my sheep... I am responsible for this flower..."

I took my rough drafts of drawings out of my pocket. The little prince looked them over, and laughed as he said:

"Your baobabs--they look a little like cabbages."

"Oh!"

I had been so proud of my baobabs!

"Your fox--his ears look a little like horns; and they are too long."

And he laughed again.

"You must keep your promise," said the little prince, softly, as he sat down beside me once more.

_____

_____

"You know--a muzzle for my sheep... I am responsible for this flower..."

_____

_____

"Your baobabs--they look a little like cabbages."

_____

_____

나도 물을 마셨다. 숨을 쉬기가 편했다. 해가 떠오르면 모래는 꿀과 같은 색이 된다. 나는 그 빛깔에도 행복해졌다. 그렇다면 슬퍼할 일이 뭐가 있단 말인가? "아저씨, 약속을 지켜야 해." 어린 왕자가 부드럽게 말했다. 그는 다시 한번 내 옆에 앉아 있었다. "무슨 약속?" "약속했잖아, 양에게 입마개를 씌워 준다고…. 난 이 꽃에 책임이 있어…." 나는 주머니에서 윤곽선만 잡아 둔 그림들을 꺼냈다. 어린 왕자는 내 그림을 보더니 웃음을 터뜨렸다. "아저씨가 그린 바오바브나무는 꼭 양배추처럼 생겼어." "이런!" 나는 내가 그린 바오바브나무에 자부심을 느끼고 있었다! "여우는 귀가 너무 길어. 꼭 뿔 같잖아." 그는 또다시 웃었다.

"You are not fair, little prince," I said. "I don't know how to draw anything except boa constrictors from the outside and boa constrictors from the inside."

"Oh, that will be all right," he said, "children understand."

So then I made a pencil sketch of a muzzle. And as I gave it to him my heart was torn.

"You have plans that I do not know about," I said.

But he did not answer me. He said to me, instead:

"You know--my descent to the earth... Tomorrow will be its anniversary."

Then, after a silence, he went on:

"I came down very near here."

And he flushed.

And once again, without understanding why, I had a queer sense of sorrow. One question, however, occurred to me:

어휘   fair 공정한   children 아이들   tear 찢다   instead ~대신에   descent 내려옴   flush
붉어지다   sorrow 슬픔   occur 생겨나다

"I don't know how to draw anything except boa constrictors from the outside and boa constrictors from the inside."

"Oh, that will be all right," he said, "children understand."

"You have plans that I do not know about," I said.

"이봐요, 어린 왕자님. 평가가 너무 박하잖아요." 내가 말했다. "전 속이 보이거나 보이지 않는 보아뱀밖에 그릴 줄 모른다고요." "오, 괜찮아." 그가 대답했다. "어린이들은 알아볼 수 있으니까." 나는 연필로 입마개를 그렸다. 그 그림을 어린 왕자에게 전해준 순간 마음이 찢어질 듯 아팠다. "넌 내가 모르는 계획을 갖고 있는 거지?" 내가 말했다. 그는 대답 대신 이렇게 말했다. "내가 지구에 내려온 지도… 내일이면 꼭 일 년이야." 잠깐의 침묵 후 그가 말을 이었다. "내가 도착한 곳은 바로 이 근처였어." 그의 얼굴이 붉어졌다. 또 한 번 이유를 알 수 없는 기묘한 슬픔이 찾아왔다. 그리고 한 가지 의문이 떠올랐다.

"Then it was not by chance that on the morning when I first met you--a week ago--you were strolling along like that, all alone, a thousand miles from any inhabited region? You were on the your back to the place where you landed?"

The little prince flushed again.

And I added, with some hesitancy:

"Perhaps it was because of the anniversary?"

The little prince flushed once more. He never answered questions--but when one flushes does that not mean "Yes"?

"Ah," I said to him, "I am a little frightened--"

But he interrupted me.

"Now you must work. You must return to your engine. I will be waiting for you here. Come back tomorrow evening..."

But I was not reassured. I remembered the fox. One runs the risk of weeping a little, if one lets himself be tamed...

어휘 by chance 우연히 stroll 걷다 inhabit 거주하다 region 지역 land 착륙하다
hesitancy 망설임 interrupt 중단 시키다 reassure 안심시키다 weep 울다

"You were on the your back to the place where you landed?"

_____

_____

"Perhaps it was because of the anniversary?"

_____

_____

One runs the risk of weeping a little, if one lets himself be tamed...

_____

_____

"그럼 일주일 전 우리가 처음 만난 날 아침, 사람이 사는 지역에서 수천 킬로미터 떨어진 곳에 네가 혼자 걷고 있었던 건 우연이 아니구나. 내려온 지점으로 다시 돌아가고 있었던 거니?" 어린 왕자는 다시 얼굴을 붉혔다. 나는 조금 망설이다가 덧붙였다. "이곳에 온 지 일 년이 되는 날이라서?" 어린 왕자는 다시 얼굴을 붉혔다. 그는 질문에 대답하는 법이 없었지만, 사람이 얼굴을 붉힐 때는 '그렇다'는 뜻이 아니던가? "아!" 나는 그에게 말했다. "내가 두려운 건…." 하지만 그가 내 말을 끊었다. "이제 아저씨는 일을 해야지. 엔진을 고쳐야 하잖아. 난 여기서 아저씨를 기다리고 있을게. 내일 저녁에 돌아오도록 해…." 하지만 나는 안심이 되지 않았다. 여우 생각이 났다. 누군가에게 길들여지면 조금 울게 될 위험이 생기는 것이다….

Beside the well there was the ruin of an old stone wall. When I came back from my work, the next evening, I saw from some distance away my little prince sitting on top of a wall, with his feet dangling. And I heard him say:

"Then you don't remember. This is not the exact spot."

Another voice must have answered him, for he replied to it:

"Yes, yes! It is the right day, but this is not the place."

I continued my walk toward the wall. At no time did I see or hear anyone. The little prince, however, replied once again:

"--Exactly. You will see where my track begins, in the sand. You have nothing to do but wait for me there. I shall be there tonight."

I was only twenty meters from the wall, and I still saw nothing.

After a silence the little prince spoke again:

"You have good poison? You are sure that it will not make me suffer too long?"

I stopped in my tracks, my heart torn asunder; but still I did not understand.

어휘 stone wall 돌담 dangle 매달리다 exact 정확한 spot 장소 track 여정 poison 독
suffer 고통 받다 tear 찢어지다 asunder 산산히 흩어진

I saw from some distance away my little prince sitting on top of a wall, with his feet dangling.

"You are sure that it will not make me suffer too long?"

I stopped in my tracks, my heart torn asunder; but still I did not understand.

우물 근처에는 폐허가 된 오래된 돌담이 하나 있었다. 다음 날 저녁 일을 하고 돌아오는 길에 멀찍이 보니, 어린 왕자가 그 위에 앉아 다리를 흔들거리고 있었다. 나는 그의 목소리를 들었다. "그럼 기억나지 않는다는 거야? 정확히 여기는 아니야." 그러더니 다른 누군가와 대화하듯이 대꾸했다. "맞아, 맞아! 날짜는 정확해. 하지만 장소가 틀렸다고." 나는 돌담을 향해 쭉 걸어갔다. 아무것도 보이거나 들리지 않았지만, 어린 왕자는 또다시 누군가에게 대답했다. "… 물론이지. 모래 위에 찍힌 내 발자국이 어디서 시작되는지 봐. 거기서 기다리면 돼. 오늘 밤 거기로 갈게." 돌담에서 20m쯤 되는 거리까지 갔지만 여전히 아무도 눈에 띄지 않았다. 잠깐의 침묵 후, 어린 왕자가 말을 이었다. "네 독은 강해? 너무 오랫동안 아프게 하지 않을 자신 있지?" 나는 그 자리에 멈춰 섰다. 가슴이 미어지는 것 같았지만, 여전히 무슨 상황인지 알 수 없었다.

"Now go away," said the little prince. "I want to get down from the wall."

I dropped my eyes, then, to the foot of the wall--and I leaped into the air. There before me, facing the little prince, was one of those yellow snakes that take just thirty seconds to bring your life to an end. Even as I was digging into my pocked to get out my revolver I made a running step back. But, at the noise I made, the snake let himself flow easily across the sand like the dying spray of a fountain, and, in no apparent hurry, disappeared, with a light metallic sound, among the stones.

어휘 get down 내려가다 drop (시선을) 떨구다 leap 뛰어오르다 snake 뱀 dig into 파헤치다 fountain 샘, 분수 apparent 눈에 보이는 disappear 사라지다

There before me, facing the little prince, was one of those yellow snakes that take just thirty seconds to bring your life to an end.

But, at the noise I made, the snake let himself flow easily across the sand like the dying spray of a fountain, and, in no apparent hurry, disappeared, with a light metallic sound, among the stones.

"이제 가 봐." 어린 왕자가 말했다. "나도 여기서 내려갈래." 나는 시선을 낮춰 돌담 아래쪽을 보았다가 깜짝 놀라서 펄쩍 뛰었다. 단 삼십 초만에 사람을 죽일 수 있는 노란 뱀 한 마리가 어린 왕자를 향해 머리를 들고 있었다. 나는 권총을 찾아 주머니를 뒤지며 서둘러 뒤로 물러났다. 그러나 내 발소리를 들은 뱀은 땅에 스며드는 물줄기처럼 모래 속을 파고들더니, 조금도 서두르는 기색 없이 가벼운 금속성 소리를 내며 돌멩이들 틈으로 사라져 버렸다.

I reached the wall just in time to catch my little man in my arms; his face was white as snow.

"What does this mean?" I demanded. "Why are you talking with snakes?"

I had loosened the golden muffler that he always wore. I had moistened his temples, and had given him some water to drink. And now I did not dare ask him any more questions. He looked at me very gravely, and put his arms around my neck. I felt his heart beating like the heart of a dying bird, shot with someone's rifle...

"I am glad that you have found what was the matter with your engine," he said. "Now you can go back home--"

"How do you know about that?"

I was just coming to tell him that my work had been successful, beyond anything that I had dared to hope.

He made no answer to my question, but he added:

"I, too, am going back home today..."

Then, sadly--

I reached the wall just in time to catch my little man in my arms; his face was white as snow.

"Why are you talking with snakes?"

He made no answer to my question, but he added: "I, too, am going back home today..."

나는 돌담 아래까지 가서 눈처럼 하얗게 질린 어린 왕자를 간신히 양팔로 받아 안았다. "대체 뭐 하는 거야?" 내가 말했다. "어째서 뱀이랑 이야기를 하는 거니?" 나는 그가 항상 두르고 있는 금빛 머플러를 푼 뒤 관자놀이에 물을 적시고 몇 모금 마시게 했다. 그쯤 되자 그에게 뭔가 물어볼 용기가 나지 않았다. 그는 심각한 표정으로 나를 바라보더니 내 목에 팔을 둘렀다. 그의 심장 박동은 꼭 사냥총에 맞아 죽어가는 새처럼 느껴졌다. "아저씨가 고장 난 엔진을 고쳐서 기뻐." 그가 말했다. "이제 집에 돌아갈 수 있는 거지?" "네가 그걸 어떻게 알았니?" 나는 생각지도 못하게 고장 난 부분을 수리해 냈고, 그 사실을 알리기 위해 그를 찾았던 것이다. 어린 왕자는 내 질문에 대답하지 않았지만 이렇게 말했다. "나도 오늘 집으로 돌아가…." 그러더니 서글픈 기색으로 덧붙였다.

"It is much farther... It is much more difficult..."

I realized clearly that something extraordinary was happening. I was holding him close in my arms as if he were a little child; and yet it seemed to me that he was rushing headlong toward an abyss from which I could do nothing to restrain him...

His look was very serious, like some one lost far away.

"I have your sheep. And I have the sheep's box. And I have the muzzle..."

And he gave me a sad smile.

I waited a long time. I could see that he was reviving little by little.

---

 farther 더 먼 clearly 분명히 extraordinary 이상한, 특별한 headlong 거꾸로
abyss 심연 restrain 저지하다 revive 되살아나다

I realized clearly that something extraordinary was happening.

His look was very serious, like some one lost far away.

"I have your sheep. And I have the sheep's box. And I have the muzzle..."

"내가 가야 할 길이 훨씬 멀고… 훨씬 어려워." 나는 뭔가 심상치 않은 일이 일어나고 있음을 깨달았다. 그를 작은 아이처럼 품에 꼭 안았지만, 그가 붙잡을 수 없는 심연 속으로 맹렬히 빨려 들어가는 느낌이 들었다. 그의 표정은 저 멀리서 방황하는 사람처럼 심각했다. "내겐 아저씨가 준 양이 있어. 양을 담아둘 상자도 있고 입마개도 있지." 그는 서글픈 미소를 띠었다. 나는 한참을 기다렸다. 그의 혈색이 조금씩 돌아오는 것이 느껴졌다.

"Dear little man," I said to him, "you are afraid..."

He was afraid, there was no doubt about that. But he laughed lightly.

"I shall be much more afraid this evening..."

Once again I felt myself frozen by the sense of something irreparable. And I knew that I could not bear the thought of never hearing that laughter any more. For me, it was like a spring of fresh water in the desert.

"Little man," I said, "I want to hear you laugh again."

But he said to me:

"Tonight, it will be a year... My star, then, can be found right above the place where I came to the Earth, a year ago..."

"Little man," I said, "tell me that it is only a bad dream--this affair of the snake, and the meeting-place, and the star..."

But he did not answer my plea. He said to me, instead:

"The thing that is important is the thing that is not seen..."

어휘 doubt 의심 frozen 얼어붙은 irreparable 돌이킬 수 없는 spring 샘 affair 사건
plea 간청

"Dear little man," I said to him, "you are afraid…"

And I knew that I could not bear the thought of never hearing that laughter any more.

For me, it was like a spring of fresh water in the desert.

"꼬마 친구." 내가 말했다. "넌 두려워하고 있구나…." 그는 분명 두려워하고 있었지만, 살며시 웃음을 보였다. "오늘 저녁엔 더 무서울 거야…." 다시 한번 영영 돌이킬 수 없는 일이 일어나리라는 예감에 몸이 얼어붙었다. 그 웃음소리를 다시는 들을 수 없다는 생각에 참을 수 없었다. 내게 그 웃음은 사막의 샘 같은 존재였다. "꼬마 친구, 네 웃음소리를 다시 듣고 싶어." 하지만 그는 내게 말했다. "오늘 밤이면 꼭 일 년이 돼. 우리 별은 내가 작년 오늘 내려왔던 그 장소 바로 위쪽에 있게 될 거야…." "꼬마 친구, 그 뱀이니 약속이니 별이니 하는 이야기는 전부 나쁜 꿈이라고 말해 줘…." 하지만 그는 내 애원에 답하지 않았다. 대신 이렇게 말할 뿐이었다. "중요한 건 눈에 보이지 않아…."

"Yes, I know..."

"It is just as it is with the flower. If you love a flower that lives on a star, it is sweet to look at the sky at night. All the stars are a-bloom with flowers..."

"Yes, I know..."

"It is just as it is with the water. Because of the pulley, and the rope, what you gave me to drink was like music. You remember--how good it was."

"Yes, I know..."

"And at night you will look up at the stars. Where I live everything is so small that I cannot show you where my star is to be found. It is better, like that. My star will just be one of the stars, for you. And so you will love to watch all the stars in the heavens... they will all be your friends. And, besides, I am going to make you a present..."

He laughed again.

어휘 know 알다 abloom 꽃이 핀 pulley 도르래 watch 바라보다 heaven 하늘
present 선물

If you love a flower that lives on a star, it is sweet to look at the sky at night.

My star will just be one of the stars, for you.

And so you will love to watch all the stars in the heavens... they will all be your friends.

"Ah, little prince, dear little prince! I love to hear that laughter!"

"That is my present. Just that. It will be as it was when we drank the water..."

"What are you trying to say?"

"All men have the stars," he answered, "but they are not the same things for different people. For some, who are travelers, the stars are guides. For others they are no more than little lights in the sky. For others, who are scholars, they are problems. For my businessman they were wealth. But all these stars are silent. You--you alone--will have the stars as no one else has them--"

"What are you trying to say?"

"In one of the stars I shall be living. In one of them I shall be laughing. And so it will be as if all the stars were laughing, when you look at the sky at night... You--only you--will have stars that can laugh!"

어휘 guide 길잡이 scholar 학자 wealth 부, 재산 silent 침묵하는 laugh 웃다

"Ah, little prince, dear little prince! I love to hear that laughter!"

"That is my present. Just that. It will be as it was when we drank the water…"

"And so it will be as if all the stars were laughing, when you look at the sky at night…"

 해 석

"아, 어린 왕자, 내 친구 어린 왕자! 난 네 웃음소리가 너무 좋아!" "그게 바로 내 선물이야. 우리가 물을 마실 때와 똑같아…." "그게 무슨 뜻이지?" "사람은 누구나 별을 볼 수 있어." 그가 말했다. "하지만 모든 이들에게 별은 각각 다른 존재지. 여행하는 사람에게 별은 길잡이야. 어떤 이에게는 그저 조그만 불빛일 뿐이고. 학자에게는 연구해야 할 대상이지. 내가 만났던 사업가에겐 별이 곧 재산이었어. 하지만 이 모든 별은 조용할 거야. 오직 아저씨만이 누구도 갖지 못한 별을 갖게 될 거야." "그게 무슨 뜻이지?" "저 별들 중 하나에서 내가 살고 있을 테니까. 그 중 하나에서 내가 웃고 있는 거야. 그러니 아저씨가 밤하늘을 올려다보면 모든 별이 웃고 있는 것처럼 보이겠지…. 오직 아저씨만이 웃을 줄 아는 별을 갖게 되는 거야!"

And he laughed again.

"And when your sorrow is comforted (time soothes all sorrows) you will be content that you have known me. You will always be my friend. You will want to laugh with me. And you will sometimes open your window, so, for that pleasure... And your friends will be properly astonished to see you laughing as you look up at the sky! Then you will say to them, 'Yes, the stars always make me laugh!' And they will think you are crazy. It will be a very shabby trick that I shall have played on you..."

And he laughed again.

"It will be as if, in place of the stars, I had given you a great number of little bells that knew how to laugh..."

And he laughed again. Then he quickly became serious:

"Tonight--you know... Do not come."

"I shall not leave you," I said.

어휘 comfort 편안하게 하다 soothe 진정시키다 sorrow 슬픔 content 만족하다
pleasure 기쁨 astonish 깜짝 놀라게 하다 shabby 못된 play on 장난치다
serious 심각한

"And when your sorrow is comforted you will be content that you have known me."

"And your friends will be properly astonished to see you laughing as you look up at the sky!"

"It will be as if, in place of the stars, I had given you a great number of little bells that knew how to laugh…"

그는 또다시 웃었다. "아저씨의 슬픔이 사그라지면(시간은 모든 슬픔을 진정시키니까) 나를 알게 되었던 걸 기뻐하게 될 거야. 아저씨는 언제까지나 내 친구야. 아저씨는 나와 함께 웃고 싶어 할 거고. 그럴 때면 기쁜 마음으로 창문을 열겠지…. 아저씨의 다른 친구들은 아저씨가 하늘을 올려다보며 웃는 걸 보고 깜짝 놀랄 거야! 그러면 아저씨는 그들에게 말하겠지. '난 별들을 볼 때마다 웃음이 나오거든!' 그들은 아저씨가 미쳤다고 생각할 거야. 그럼 난 아저씨에게 못된 짓을 한 셈이 되는 건가…." 그는 또다시 웃었다. "난 아저씨에게 별 대신에 웃을 줄 아는 조그만 방울들을 잔뜩 준 거야." 그는 또다시 웃었다. 하지만 이내 심각한 표정이 되었다. "오늘 밤에는… 오지 마." "난 네 곁을 떠나지 않을 거야." 내가 말했다.

"I shall look as if I were suffering. I shall look a little as if I were dying. It is like that. Do not come to see that. It is not worth the trouble…"

"I shall not leave you."

But he was worried.

"I tell you--it is also because of the snake. He must not bite you. Snakes--they are malicious creatures. This one might bite you just for fun…"

"I shall not leave you."

But a thought came to reassure him:

"It is true that they have no more poison for a second bite."

That night I did not see him set out on his way. He got away from me without making a sound. When I succeeded in catching up with him he was walking along with a quick and resolute step. He said to me merely:

"Ah! You are there…"

And he took me by the hand. But he was still worrying.

어휘   suffering 고통받는   leave 떠나다   bite 물다   malicious 심술궂은   creature 존재
catch up 따라잡다   resolute 확고한   merely 그저, 단지

That night I did not see him set out on his way.

He got away from me without making a sound.

When I succeeded in catching up with him he was walking along with a quick and resolute step.

"난 아픈 것처럼 보일 거야. 최소한 죽어가는 사람처럼 보일 거야. 내가 하려는 것은 그런 거거든. 그 모습을 보러 오지 마. 그럴 가치가 없어…." "난 네 곁을 떠나지 않을 거야." 하지만 그는 나를 걱정했다. "내가 이런 말을 하는 건 뱀 때문이기도 해. 아저씨를 물면 안 되니까. 뱀들은 심술궂은 생물이야. 그저 장난삼아 아저씨를 물지도 몰라…." "난 네 곁을 떠나지 않을 거야." 그는 무슨 생각이 들었는지 안심하는 기색이 되었다. "그래도 두 번째 물 때는 독이 없으니까." 그날 밤, 나는 그가 길을 나서는 모습을 보지 못했다. 그는 소리 없이 사라져 버렸다. 겨우 그를 따라잡았을 때, 그는 빠르고 확고한 걸음으로 걸어가고 있었다. 그가 내게 말했다. "아, 왔구나…." 그는 내 손을 잡았다. 하지만 여전히 내 걱정을 하고 있었다.

"It was wrong of you to come. You will suffer. I shall look as if I were dead; and that will not be true..."

I said nothing.

"You understand... it is too far. I cannot carry this body with me. It is too heavy."

I said nothing.

"But it will be like an old abandoned shell. There is nothing sad about old shells..."

I said nothing.

He was a little discouraged. But he made one more effort:

"You know, it will be very nice. I, too, shall look at the stars. All the stars will be wells with a rusty pulley. All the stars will pour out fresh water for me to drink..."

I said nothing.

"That will be so amusing! You will have five hundred million little bells, and I shall have five hundred million springs of fresh water..."

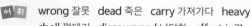

어휘 wrong 잘못 dead 죽은 carry 가져가다 heavy 무거운 abandon 버리다
shell 껍데기 discouraged 낙담한 effort 노력 rusty 녹슨

"I shall look as if I were dead; and that will not be true…"

"All the stars will be wells with a rusty pulley."

"You will have five hundred million little bells, and I shall have five hundred million springs of fresh water…"

"여기 온 건 아저씨 잘못이야. 아저씨는 아파하게 될 거야. 내가 죽은 것처럼 보일 테니까. 하지만 그건 진짜가 아니야…" 나는 아무 말도 하지 않았다. "이해할 수 있지? 우리 별은 너무 멀어서…. 이 몸을 가지고는 갈 수 없어. 너무 무겁거든." 나는 아무 말도 하지 않았다. "그건 벗어던진 낡은 껍데기와 같아. 낡은 껍데기를 보고 슬퍼할 이유는 없어…" 나는 아무 말도 하지 않았다. 그는 약간 풀이 죽은 것 같았지만 애써 말을 이었다. "있잖아. 굉장히 좋을 거야. 나도 별들을 바라볼 거거든. 내게는 모든 별이 샘과 녹슨 도르래를 품고 있는 것처럼 보일 거야. 모든 별이 내게 맑은 물을 퍼 올려 줄 거고." 나는 아무 말도 하지 않았다. "재미있을 거야! 아저씨는 오억 개의 작은 방울을 갖게 되고, 나는 맑은 물이 솟는 오억 개의 우물을 갖게 되고…."

And he too said nothing more, because he was crying...

"Here it is. Let me go on by myself."

And he sat down,

because he was afraid.

 Then he said, again:

"You know--my flower...

I am responsible for her. And she is so weak! She is so naïve! She has four thorns, of no use at all, to protect herself against all the world..."

I too sat down, because I was not able to stand up any longer.

"There now--that is all..."

He still hesitated a little; then he got up. He took one step. I could not move.

go on 계속하다 by myself 혼자 afraid 두려워하는 responsible for ~에 책임이 있는
naïve 순진한 protect 보호하다 hesitate 망설이다 move 움직이다

"You know--my flower... I am responsible for her."

"She has four thorns, of no use at all, to protect herself against all the world..."

I too sat down, because I was not able to stand up any longer.

그때부터는 어린 왕자도 말이 없어졌다. 울고 있었던 것이다. "여기야. 이제 나 혼자 하게 해줘." 그는 자리에 앉았다. 두려움을 느낀 것이다. 그가 다시 입을 열었다. "아저씨. 나는 내 꽃에게… 그녀에게 책임이 있어. 게다가 그 꽃은 몹시 약하거든! 순진하기도 하고! 온 세상에 맞설 무기라곤 쓸모도 없는 가시 네 개뿐이지." 나는 더 이상 서 있을 수가 없어서 그와 함께 앉았다. "지금이야…. 이제 끝이야." 그는 여전히 망설이고 있었지만 얼마 후 몸을 일으켜 한 발자국 나아갔다. 나는 움직일 수 없었다.

There was nothing but a flash of yellow close to his ankle. He remained motionless for an instant. He did not cry out. He fell as gently as a tree falls. There was not even any sound, because of the sand.

어휘 flash 불빛   close to ~에 가까운   ankle 발목   remain ~한 상태로 남아 있다
motionless 움직이지 않는   instant 순간   cry ot 소리를 지르다   fall 쓰러지다

There was nothing but a flash of yellow close to his ankle.

He fell as gently as a tree falls.

There was not even any sound, because of the sand.

그의 발목 근처에서 노란 불빛이 반짝인 것뿐이었다. 그는 잠시 그대로 서 있었다. 소리를 지르지는 않았다. 그저 나무가 쓰러지듯 살포시 쓰러졌다. 모래밭 위였기에 소리조차 나지 않았다.

And now six years have already gone by... I have never yet told this story. The companions who met me on my return were well content to see me alive. I was sad, but I told them: "I am tired."

Now my sorrow is comforted a little. That is to say--not entirely. But I know that he did go back to his planet, because I did not find his body at daybreak. It was not such a heavy body... and at night I love to listen to the stars. It is like five hundred million little bells...

But there is one extraordinary thing... when I drew the muzzle for the little prince, I forgot to add the leather strap to it. He will never have been able to fasten it on his sheep. So now I keep wondering: what is happening on his planet? Perhaps the sheep has eaten the flower...

---

 go by (시간이) 흐르다　companion 친구　return 귀환　content 기뻐하다　comfort 편안해지다　entirely 완전히　daybreak 동틀 무렵　leather strap 가죽끈　fasten 고정 시키다

And now six years have already gone by... I have never yet told this story.

Now my sorrow is comforted a little. That is to say--not entirely.

But I know that he did go back to his planet, because I did not find his body at daybreak.

그 뒤로 벌써 육 년의 세월이 흘렀다…. 나는 지금껏 이 이야기를 한 번도 꺼내지 않았다. 다시 만난 친구들은 내가 무사히 살아 돌아온 데 기뻐했다. 나는 슬픔을 감춘 채 '피곤하다'고 말했다. 이제는 내 슬픔도 조금은 사그라졌다. 그러니까… 완전히 사그라진 건 아니라는 얘기다. 하지만 나는 그가 자기 별로 돌아갔다는 사실을 안다. 해 뜰 무렵 그의 몸을 찾지 못했기 때문이다. 그렇게 무거운 몸은 아니었으니…. 나는 밤마다 별들의 소리에 귀 기울이길 좋아하게 되었다. 별들은 오억 개의 작은 방울처럼 느껴졌다…. 그런데 묘한 일이 있다. 어린 왕자에게 입마개를 그려 주었을 때, 깜빡하고 가죽끈을 달아 주지 않았던 것이다. 어린 왕자로서는 입마개를 양의 주둥이에 잡아맬 도리가 없다. 그 사실은 내게 끊임없는 궁금증을 가져온다. 그의 별에서 무슨 일이 일어났을까? 어쩌면 양이 꽃을 먹어버렸을지도 몰라….

At one time I say to myself: "Surely not! The little prince shuts his flower under her glass globe every night, and he watches over his sheep very carefully..." Then I am happy. And there is sweetness in the laughter of all the stars.

But at another time I say to myself: "At some moment or other one is absentminded, and that is enough! On some one evening he forgot the glass globe, or the sheep got out, without making any noise, in the night..." And then the little bells are changed to tears...

Here, then, is a great mystery. For you who also love the little prince, and for me, nothing in the universe can be the same if somewhere, we do not know where, a sheep that we never saw has--yes or no?--eaten a rose...

어휘 shut ~을 가두어 넣다   carefully 신중하게   absentminded 방심한   get out 나오다
noise 소리   tear 눈물

"The little prince shuts his flower under her glass globe every night, and he watches over his sheep very carefully..."

"At some moment or other one is absentminded, and that is enough!"

And then the little bells are changed to tears...

어떤 때는 이런 생각이 든다. '그럴 리가! 어린 왕자가 꽃을 매일 밤 유리 덮개로 잘 덮어 두었을 거야. 양도 잘 지킬 테지.' 그런 날은 기분이 좋다. 그러면 모든 별이 달콤하게 웃는 것처럼 보인다. 하지만 어떤 때는 다른 생각도 든다. '한두 번 깜빡할 수도 있잖아. 그러면 끝장인데! 어느 날 저녁 유리 덮개를 씌우지 않거나 양이 밤중에 발소리를 죽이고 울타리를 벗어났을지도 몰라……' 그런 날은 작은 방울들이 모두 눈물로 변한다. 정말이지 신비로운 일이다. 내게, 혹은 어린 왕자를 사랑하는 여러분에게, 실제로 본 적도 없고 어디 있는지도 모를 양 한 마리가 장미를 먹었느냐 말았느냐 하는 문제가 세상에서 가장 중요한 일이 되다니….

Look up at the sky. Ask yourselves: is it yes or no? Has the sheep eaten the flower? And you will see how everything changes...

And no grown-up will ever understand that this is a matter of so much importance!

This is, to me, the loveliest and saddest landscape in the world. It is the same as that on the preceding page, but I have drawn it again to impress it on your memory. It is here that the little prince appeared on Earth, and disappeared.

여휘 look up 올려다보다 landscape 풍경 preceding ~에 앞선 impress 새겨지다
memory 기억 appear 나타나다 disappear 사라지다

Look up at the sky. Ask yourselves: is it yes or no?

It is the same as that on the preceding page, but I have drawn it again to impress it on your memory.

It is here that the little prince appeared on Earth, and disappeared.

 석

하늘을 바라보고 마음속으로 물어보라. 양이 꽃을 먹었을까? 먹지 않았을까? 그 대답에 따라 모든 것이 달라질 것이다. 그런데 어떤 어른도 이것이 그토록 중요한 문제임을 이해하지 못한다! 이것은 내게 세상에서 가장 아름답고도 슬픈 풍경이다. 바로 앞 장에서 본 것과 똑같은 풍경이지만, 여러분의 기억에 분명히 새기기 위해 한 번 더 그렸다. 어린 왕자는 바로 이곳에서, 지구에 나타났다가 사라졌다.

Look at it carefully so that you will be sure to recognize it in case you travel some day to the African desert. And, if you should come upon this spot, please do not hurry on. Wait for a time, exactly under the star. Then, if a little man appears who laughs, who has golden hair and who refuses to answer questions, you will know who he is. If this should happen, please comfort me. Send me word that he has come back.

어휘 look at ~를 보다 carefully 신중하게 recognize 알아보다 spot 장소 hurry on 서두르다 refuse 거부하다 comfort 편안하게 하다 send word 알리다

Look at it carefully so that you will be sure to recognize it in case you travel some day to the African desert.

Then, if a little man appears who laughs, who has golden hair and who refuses to answer questions, you will know who he is.

Send me word that he has come back.

이 그림을 잘 보아 두었다가 언젠가 아프리카 사막을 여행할 때 마주치면 알아볼 수 있길 바란다. 만약 이 풍경을 마주한다면, 서두르지 말고 별들 아래 잠시만 기다려 보길 부탁한다. 그때 금빛 머리에 웃음을 머금은 채 질문에 대답하지 않는 작은 소년이 나타난다면, 여러분은 그가 누구인지 알아볼 것이다. 그런 일이 일어난다면 부디 내게 호의를 베풀어, 그가 돌아왔다는 소식을 전해 주길 부탁한다.